Girldrive

girl drive

Criss-Crossing America, Redefining Feminism

Nona Willis Aronowitz & Emma Bee Bernstein
Foreword by Jennifer Baumgardner

Girldrive

Criss-Crossing America, Redefining Feminism

Copyright © 2009 by Emma Bee Bernstein & Nona Willis Aronowitz

Published by
Seal Press
A Member of the Perseus Books Group
1700 Fourth Street | Berkeley, California | 94710

Library of Congress Cataloging-in-Publication Data

Bernstein, Emma Bee, 1985–
    Girldrive : criss-crossing America, redefining feminism / by Emma Bee Bernstein & Nona Willis Aronowitz.
        p.   cm.
    Includes bibliographical references and index.
    ISBN 978-1-58005-273-3 (alk. paper)
    1. Feminism—United States. I. Willis Aronowitz, Nona, 1984–
II. Title.
    HQ1421.B475 2009
    305.420973'090511—dc22
                2009014217

Cover & interior design by Kate Basart/Union Pageworks
Cover photo credits, clockwise from Washington State: Puja © Emma Bee Bernstein; Nona in North Carolina © Emma Bee Bernstein; Mehiko © Emma Bee Bernstein; Pia © Sadye Vassil; Mari, fear and loathing–style © Emma Bee Bernstein; chatting at Cha Cha © Emma Bee Bernstein; Raine © Emma Bee Bernstein; Julie B. © Emma Bee Bernstein; Noel © Emma Bee Bernstein; Lenelle performing at Goddard College © Vanessa Vargas; Emma in Tusayan © Marianna McClellan.
Authors photos © Beth at Eden Photography

Printed in China through Colorcraft Ltd., Hong Kong
Distributed by Publishers Group West

For two kick-ass feminists who left this world too early—,

Emma Bee Bernstein, my intellectual soulmate, whose biggest strength
and weakness was feeling everything like a stab in the heart,

and my mom, Ellen Willis, whose amazing life and jarring death was
what inspired the Girldrive adventure in the first place.

Contents

Foreword

While I was in college, before Anita Hill was cross-examined by the Senate but after I knew without a doubt I was a feminist, I remember feeling electrified by the radicals of the '60s and '70s women's movement. Their anger was mine; their books (*Dialectic of Sex*, *This Bridge*) my bibles. Their mantras became mine, too. "Well, the personal is political," I'd say at meetings of my campus women's group, inspired if not entirely firm about what that meant. "We are clicking-things-into-place-angry, because we have suddenly and shockingly perceived the basic disorder in what has been believed to be the natural order of things"—a line from "The Housewife's Moment of Truth," a 1972 article by Jane O'Reilly—showed up in the first issue of a zine I created with friends in 1991.

I may have quoted these words as if cutting open my own vein, but what wasn't mine—and it took me years to understand this—was the context in which the feminists of the '60s and '70s came up with these insights. I actually wasn't a housewife, despite the way O'Reilly's words excited me. The world had changed, opening up new territory for women, and it was up to my generation of feminists—to me?!—to inhabit that territory and figure out what feminism meant right now. To recreate the past, however glorious, was the coward's way out.

I thought about that exhilarating journey from grateful feminist heiress to woman with my own mission as I read *Girldrive*. It was daunting to step out from under the radical comfort of a world created by a previous generation. I thought about how I might not have been able to had I not talked to my peers, and especially had I not found a trusted, inspiring ally (in my case, Amy Richards).

Nona and Emma, fifteen years my juniors, undertook *Girldrive* to make sense of feminism for *their* generation. If anything, Nona and Emma had more reasons to be daunted than I did: their actual mothers are significant figures in the women's movement. But they also had more reasons to be brave because of the confidence and sense of potential that was their birthright as daughters of the second wave.

Their journey begins with a brainstorm ("We should go on a road trip!") over eggs and Bloody Marys during one of their epic girlfriend brunches. It begins, also, with death: Nona has lost her mother, brilliant writer Ellen Willis, and soon after Emma's grandfather dies. The project ends with a heartbreaking, troubling loss, too. But throughout the hundreds of interviews, it is Nona and Emma's friendship—their interest in talking to each other, the fact that each has found an intellectual and political muse—that enables incredible gains. Their friendship drives them to criss-cross the United States in a Chevy Cavalier, and really listen to women—and men—talk about feminism. By the time *Girldrive* was over, I was relating to Nona and Emma fully, realizing how much my story was similar to theirs, as well as how much it isn't. As for the latter, I am grateful for the insights into the ways in which feminism is being remade right now.

Throughout this project, Nona and Emma work hard to maintain connections across generations while still letting go of received wisdom—even the healthy and righteous received wisdom of feminism. Their interview with Kathleen Hanna, now in her forties, who was a creator of *Riot Grrrl*, is illustrative. "Kathleen wants women to learn who they are as activists," they conclude. "And after butting their heads against some of the same problems of the past, 'they will hopefully be able to move forward.' . . . . What [Hanna] hopes is what we've been talking about—that this half-forgotten history learned from our mothers and mentors does not discourage us; that it instead pushes us forward to talk to our generation—productively."

What could be more productive than turning off one's computer, getting into a car, and actually going to find people whose lives intersect with feminism? What could be more productive than creating this record of those meetings for those who wonder what young people are thinking or doing to push gender justice forward?

When I closed this book, I wanted to get in my car with my best friend and hit the road. If you feel the same way, I say *go, go, go*. I can't wait for more reports from the future of feminism.

—**Jennifer Baumgardner**
New York City, May 2009

Introduction

The story of *Girldrive* begins with eggs and Bloody Marys. Emma and I were having one of our three-hour brunches, a tradition that started a few years ago when we left to go to colleges nine hundred miles away from each other and could only hang out during vacations. We'd been friends since we were eleven years old. We met at Camp Kinderland and both came from the same bubble: the liberal Jewish one that inhabits New York's Upper West Side and Greenwich Village. We had one of those friendships where we wouldn't talk for months, and then it would feel like no time had passed when we'd finally make a point to get together—which in our later years usually included meeting up at random dive bars for whiskey sours, or our occasional brunch dates on hungover mornings.

This particular Sunday wasn't a typical catch-up sesh. In a sudden acceleration of gradually creeping lung cancer, my mom, Ellen Willis, a well-known feminist writer, had died a couple weeks earlier. Emma had been in the thick of her finals at the University of Chicago and hadn't been able to come to the funeral, so she made it her first order of business to see me over Thanksgiving. I told her about the outpouring of feminist love I had received—from my mom's friends, students, and anonymous admirers. It was like a crash

course in feminism and its endless definitions. Emma, meanwhile, was fresh from the Feminist Future symposium at the Museum of Modern Art, where she'd recently been sucked into a whirlpool of several generations of feminists for three days straight. She'd come away with the observation that the relationships between young women like her and older feminists wavered between inspiration and disconnect. So we'd both been confronted with the legacy of feminism head-on, and there was no denying that this word, this history, this *feeling* meant something to us.

The way we saw it, being feminists meant being conscious of and angry about gender injustice—from unequal pay and domestic violence to slut-shaming and the lack of paid maternity leave. It meant believing in the right to freedom, safety, and pleasure. It meant understanding how gender intertwines with race, class, and politics. It meant educating ourselves about the many incarnations of feminism and building on each one's progress. To us, it was a tool, a code word, and a state of mind. We both grew up with stridently feminist moms, knew a lot about feminism's history, and had no problems calling ourselves feminists.

This was our reality, but we had no idea what other women around the country were thinking, women who didn't post on blogs or put themselves in the media's spotlight. We wanted to seek out the opinions of our generation—young women whose future was raw and indeterminate; women who were independent, thoughtful, fun-loving, and motivated; women who were kicking ass and changing the world. We were dying to know: What do other twentysomething women care about? What are their hopes, worries, and ambitions? Have they heard of this nebulous idea of "feminism," and do they relate to it?

We were on our third Bloody when Emma blurted out, "Let's go on a road trip! You're a writer. I'm a photographer. Let's write a book; let's do a project. Let's fucking *do something!*"

A road trip seemed like a perfect plan. Not only would it give us a chance to talk face-to-face to women our age from different cities, back-grounds, religions, and professions but it would also allow us to photograph these women in their own spaces. It would also be a time for self-discovery, a break from the blur of our lives in order to figure out what we truly wanted—which, to us, was what feminism was all about. Most of all, it would obviously be a total blast.

Based solely on the idea, we managed to find an agent, who bluntly told us, "Nobody's going to give two unknown twenty-two-year-olds a book deal without anything to show for it. You have to take a risk. You have to just *go.*" So we prepared to do just that. We started saving and planning, working shitty jobs around the clock to fund our adventure. We sent emails out to hundreds of people, asking them to spread the word, eventually hearing from women three or four degrees of separation away. When our email blasts didn't reach certain demographics, we sought them out ourselves. Later, we decided to also track down older, influential feminists we admired to get their take on our generation. After all, how could we determine the future of feminism if we didn't talk to women who had made it their life's work?

By August 2007, we had compiled a list of over two hundred women to talk to. Their knowledge of feminism ranged from none at all to being the focus of their lives. While interviewing in cities, we spontaneously contacted other women whom our interviewees recommended on the spot. When our blog started to gain popularity, we began to get contacted by women all over America inviting *us* to come interview *them*.

A week into our trip, it became apparent that using "feminism" to start a conversation didn't work for everyone. Some women's faces would go blank when we brought up the word, but would later light up when we'd ask, "What pisses you off about being a woman?" or, "What keeps you up nights?" Others couldn't get past the term's loaded meaning, dwelling on its fraught history rather than relating it to their own experience. In *Girldrive*, Emma and I make no secret of the fact that the concept of feminism was central to our lives. But we also never pretend that all women will or should get behind the same word or issue, given the vastly different lives we lead. Feminism made sense to us, so we used it as a framework to talk about the way we view our lives as young women—but if it wasn't vibing, we tried something else.

Girldrive is an assemblage of reporting, photos, and personal impressions that documents this journey we took in the fall of 2007 and into 2008. This book allows gutsy young women across the American landscape to be seen and heard. It evaluates, through an intergenerational dialogue, the current state of feminism and its many definitions. It's about the past and the present, and it glimmers on the future. It's about the promise of the open road. It's about how young women grapple with the concepts of freedom, equality, joy, ambition, sex, and love—whether they call it "feminism" or not.

Navigating Girldrive

This book is not a definitive guide to contemporary feminism. In fact, it is redefinition in its purest form—a continuation of an open-ended, fluid conversation. Emma and I chose to simply lay our evidence out on the table and mostly let our peers and she-roes speak for themselves. *Girldrive* can be read cover-to-cover, or it can be browsed through like an anthology or a magazine. Most of the vignettes stand on their own; the same

goes for each of the chapters, which are divided by region and track the route we took across the United States. Reading the text in between our reportage reveals Emma's and my personal journey, a search for freedom and purpose propelled by our restlessness and budding self-awareness.

Although I did most of the writing and Emma took most of the photos, there are instances where we switched roles—and there was quite a lot of writing (especially from Chapter 8 on) that I ended up, unexpectedly, doing on my own after Emma's untimely death. Everything that was written by Emma is marked with her byline; you will see a handful of photos accredited to me and other people (for those photos in which Emma appears, or where one of her images didn't turn out and we needed to call on our interviewees for replacements).

Chapter 10, chronicling our time in New York City, is a lot longer than the other chapters, for a few reasons. One, New York is a feminist hot spot. Many notable feminists have settled there precisely because of the like-minded community the city has to offer. Two, we were born there. Our networks reached far and wide, and people we'd known forever came through for us hardcore. Three, we had time. We spent several weeks in New York during the winter holidays, which was a far cry from the touch-and-go nature of our whirlwind national tour. But none of this means that we valued the voices of New York women more than those of women from any other city. If this were true, we would have never hit the road in the first place.

Most of our peers are introduced by their first names, while public figures (younger or older) are referred to by their full name. Many of the younger women preferred this, and I think it emphasizes the informal feeling of the conversations we had with our peers. This format is not meant to somehow elevate the opinions of more famous women.

Throughout our travels, we were asked this question a lot: Why didn't you include more rural women? This was quite simply a time, money, and efficiency issue. Given our budget, we needed to stop amid the densest populations of young women we could find. But feel free to conduct a *Girldrive Part II* that hits up all those rural pockets we missed! I'm sure it would add a-whole-nother layer to the *Girldrive* adventure.

The Ladies Behind the Wheel

Emma and I are from roughly the same political and social backgrounds, but our similarities end there. Our collaboration is truly yin and yang: I am the reporter, the investigator, the historian, the one with the burning questions. Emma was the artist, the aesthete, the romantic, the visual interpreter. While I was toiling away at profiles and concise arguments, Emma had her nose buried in her diary—scrawling half-sentences, observing cosmic connections—or was busy snapping her camera.

We came to feminism and our sense of femaleness through different avenues. Until college, I never used the word feminism, even though I was all for women's rights and always saw the connection between gender and politics. I was a girl who started shaving her legs at age ten, a teenager who watched MTV and wore push-up bras and flared Mudd Jeans, a college student who had many male lovers and friends. Despite my criticisms of it, I saw the value in inhabiting the mainstream. Even though I (usually) wouldn't put up with any sexist bullshit, I was never a misfit or a radical. But since my mom was a feminist and yet never said a critical word about my miniskirts or hip-hop CDs, I never thought that any of what I did or how I lived in the world was in contradiction with feminism, as long as I was a self-aware and thoughtful person. The feminist concepts I read about in books and on the web gradually started to make sense, and I embraced them.

Emma was punkier and rebellious, more avant garde and blasé. Unlike me, she had dabbled in feminist activism when she was young. She looked to Nan Goldin, Diane Arbus, Frida Kahlo, and Sylvia Plath as some of her artistic idols. She also found a role model in Kathleen Hanna, who helped form Third Wave feminism's Riot Grrrl movement in the early 1990s. There was something about Hanna's incendiary call to action—"Revolution grrrl style now!"—that ignited Emma's love for pink hair and fishnet tights, that led her to adopt a style rejecting ideals of body image and taking on sexuality and aggressiveness while elbowing through a sea of testosterone. Emma eventually grew out of her punk phase and became disillusioned with the girls-against-boys mentality of "sisterhood." But she began to identify with feminism again when she found herself drawn to the work of feminist scholars, artists, and photographers during her senior year of college.

We each brought our separate perspectives along for the ride, and by the end of our road trip we knew that the politics of feminism could not be separated from more intangible connections to beauty, life, and each other. I had tackled the voyage with my journalistic curiosity and yearning for the truth; Emma's experience was imbued by her keen sense of pure, euphoric lyricism. We had created a bridge between the logical and the intuitive. We had started the project on opposite sides of the spectrum and had ended up hopelessly intertwined.

Never in my wildest dreams did I imagine that I would be writing this introduction alone. This same desperate thirst for passion later drove Emma to self-destruction and madness. It was an inexplicable force that resulted in her ending her own life in Venice, Italy, in December 2008, at the Peggy Guggenheim Collection, when we were knee-deep in the *Girldrive* manuscript. The first couple weeks after her death, I felt betrayed and listless, like the verve behind *Girldrive* had been irreparably damaged. But I ultimately realized that it was exactly the opposite—that finishing *Girldrive* would prove more than ever that utopianism can prevail over very real tragedy. Emma's despair was in spite of her high hopes for feminism and her utter dedication to making the world a better place for young women. Emma battled with depression that ultimately killed her, but that cannot overshadow the fact that she was, at core, a fervently idealistic soul.

It is the same idealism that permeates *Girldrive*, a feeling that you, the reader, will surely pick up on as you follow our journey through the country. My hope is that *Girldrive* will have a ripple effect—that it will get your wheels turning, that it will get you thinking and talking about the pressing questions that come alive in these pages. If you find one vignette, one issue, even one sentence in this book that sparks a conversation or gets you off your ass to work toward what you believe in, then we will have achieved with *Girldrive* exactly what we set out to do.

—*Nona, spring 2009*

Chicago
LUCY AND ANTONIA

Twin Cities
MARIA

Detroit
ZOE AND ALEJANDRA
ISIS AND VIOLETA
CARMEN AND SARAH

Flint
MELODEE AND KRYSTAL

Ypsilanti
MARTHA AND MARIA

CHAPTER 1 — **Taking the Wheel**

CHICAGO

It is early in the morning on October 11—Eleanor Roosevelt's birthday—and I have just left New York with no clear idea of when I will return. I am headed west to Chicago in my Chevy Cavalier to meet Emma before our journey. Just a few days ago we decided last-minute to schedule a "test run" to the Twin Cities before we *really* leave to drive northwest to Wyoming. My head floods with what lies ahead: adventure, flat tires, epiphanies, wrong directions, freedom, fear; my twelve-hour drive to Chicago is a blur of future fantasies. Finally, jittery from anticipation and gas station coffee, I park my car on Emma's street. *This is going to be one long week,* I think.

Lucy and Antonia

A few hours after I arrive in Chicago, Emma and I meet up with Lucy and Antonia at Sigara, a hookah bar in Ukrainian Village. Lucy and Toni are Emma's and my respective best friends and two of our future companions on different sections of the road trip. Lucy went to Wesleyan with me. She's a Chicago native working for a postproduction house, but she wants to be a filmmaker and screenwriter. Antonia just graduated from the University of Chicago with Emma and got a job working for an advertising agency—even though art history is her real passion. Because of Antonia's doe-eyed stare and porcelain features, she has long been Emma's photographic muse.

We decide to bounce ideas off of our best girls. "What do you guys think of this project?" we ask. Both nod vigorously in support. "I like it!" Lucy exclaims in her breathy singsong. "Who doesn't like to just hang out and talk with other women?"

"But what about feminism?" I venture. Even though Emma and I had been thinking about *Girldrive* for months, we still weren't in the habit of discussing the F-word with our friends. Lucy shrugs and asks, "How can you be a woman and not be a feminist? To me being a feminist is not ignoring the fact that if you're a woman you experience things a certain way, no matter what— whether you want to face it or not."

Antonia tells us about an art project she's doing that she thinks is related. For the last few months, she's been going to strip clubs and sketching the dancers, often chatting with them as well. She tells us that she relates to these women—not only when they are having a "manufactured intimate moment," but also when she feels her own body being objectified by men. Antonia thinks that women's awareness of their beauty and the pleasure men get out of it has both positive and negative effects on women. She adds, "I think both sexes are complicit in this dynamic."

These words and questions ignite good conversation, but we wonder if we will feel the same spark with dozens of strangers in the months ahead of us.

EMMA, NONA, AND LUCY (TOP);
LUCY AND ANTONIA (BOTTOM)

NIGHT OVER BEERS

The night before Emma and I set out to start *Girldrive*, the adventure we'd been plotting for a year, we meet at the California Clipper in Humboldt Park, Chicago, for a couple beers. The Clipper is an oasis among the clutter of to-do lists that have been overtaking our brains during this insane week of planning. Things have been hard lately. I just left New York behind, and Emma's grandpa suddenly is dying. Both of us have had moneymoneymoney issues, despite working like crazy to save. We are both going through nauseating breakups. Preparing for two months on the road has been an uphill battle.

And yet, these are the things we've been consumed by: buying digital recorders and a 2008 atlas and a portable iPod charger and a cheapie $60 BlackBerry on eBay. Here we are writing hundreds of emails to women we've never met. Here I am, in a new city, about to search out dozens more. We're really doing this—all by ourselves.

Emma and I recount the summer's painful moments over beer, and each of us confesses that people have been coaxing us to postpone *Girldrive*. "Just tell Emma it's not the right time. She'll understand," one of my friends had said. "I don't get it. Why don't you and Nona wait a year for a grant to come along?" one of her friends had offered. We recall moments where we'd said to ourselves, Fuck it. We can't just take off. Our lives are too complicated. It's too scary to come back utterly penniless. But then we'd each shaken those thoughts off and kept planning.

We make a toast with our $2.00 Pabsts and clasp our hands together, like a scene in some corny movie. It is a tiny moment where we realize that this is the perfect time for the trip. We are about to take on the biggest challenge of our lives, and it's too late to let anything get in the way.

TWIN CITIES

We pack our car for the prevoyage—a condensed tour of Minneapolis and St. Paul—with a few of our friends from Chicago. We don't quite get the rush of the road as expected, which probably has to do with being squashed into a tiny car for hours on end with five people. With the exception of an amazing excursion to a Wisconsin cheese mill, we power through the trip quickly and arrive late at night. In the morning we officially kick off *Girldrive* with our first interview with a lady after Emma's own heart—a girl with a soft spot for the '90s underground feminist punk movement, Riot Grrrl.

MARIA

Maria

We meet Maria, twenty-four, for breakfast at a crunchy organic co-op. Maria is originally from Texas, from a matriarchal middle-class Mexican family. She organized Ladyfest (a women's music festival with many urban incarnations) in Denton, Texas, founded Film Fatale (a festival featuring exclusively women's films), and recently started GirlBad, a monthly showcase of women rock bands. But she doesn't call herself a feminist because "it boxes you in." She notes that like a secret code, "feminism" can be used among friends that "are down" and don't subscribe to popular myths like angry, hairy-armpitted lesbians.

But Maria does get turned off by the 1970s Second Wave aesthetic because, in her words, "it's not threatening enough." In her high school years she found Riot Grrrl music to be an empowering update, if not the answer, to the touchy-feeliness of the Second Wave. Her number one goal is to give girls a space in the music industry, to "change dude-rock," and to force men in the industry to be more progressive.

We shift from music to family, and Maria exposes one of her inner battles: the contradiction between Catholicism and feminism. She appreciates Catholicism for the same reason she seems to like girl rock bands—for the straightforward way in which beliefs are presented. Raised Catholic since birth, she tells us she's not about to stop the "the routine of traditions" pervading her household. "I'm still going to serve the men drinks when they come over to my house," she asserts. "It's just being gracious; in Mexican culture it's not seen as being disrespected."

—**Emma**

FALL

The Twin Cities are gorgeous,
quintessentially Midwestern . . .

The sky is full of the whitest
light, despite layers and layers
of clouds, making the whole
city bright and spacious . . .

The air is brisk and fresh and
cracked orange leaves pile along the pavement . . .

It is truly fall.

DETROIT

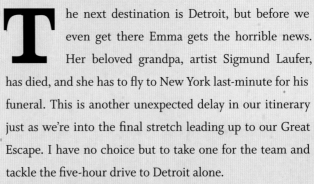

The next destination is Detroit, but before we even get there Emma gets the horrible news. Her beloved grandpa, artist Sigmund Laufer, has died, and she has to fly to New York last-minute for his funeral. This is another unexpected delay in our itinerary just as we're into the final stretch leading up to our Great Escape. I have no choice but to take one for the team and tackle the five-hour drive to Detroit alone.

I'll be staying with Elena, an incredible, warm soul who runs a worker's center at the auto plant and is about to start a PhD in Chicana studies—a degree that's only offered at two universities in the country. When I get there, Elena informs me that Detroit's women are fascinating, tough as nails, and gritty, much like their deteriorating home city. There's a kind of urgency and bluntness to Elena, a feeling of "Don't mess with us. This city is hurting, but we won't let it die." I immediately feel like I'm in good hands.

Zoe and Alejandra

My first interviewees are Elena's nineteen-year-old twin daughters, Zoe and Alejandra, whom I talk with separately in Elena's ramshackle, colorful, and book-filled abode. Zoe is demure and dressed funky. Friendly, but understated. She works at the library and is mulling over whether she's going to go back to school. She writes and does art "as an outlet," she says.

Zoe first learned about feminism at a red-leaning, hippie summer camp in Dalton, Michigan. She believes in equality for women, so in that sense she's a feminist, but she points out, "I could only define feminism when I went someplace white. People in my neighborhood never use the word. Feminism is seen as a bourgeois thing."

Shortly after I speak with Zoe, Alejandra comes home from class. She is a student at Wayne State and is in the middle of writing a young adult novel about vampires. She lived in L.A. at one point to go to beauty school but felt guilty and came back. "Detroit needs a lot of help," she tells me. "I didn't feel satisfied out there."

> ## "I could only define feminism when I went someplace white." —Zoe

Alejandra doesn't identify herself with feminism because, she says, "I agree with the concepts, but I don't do anything active to keep them. I conform to my gender and have never really questioned it." Like Zoe, she questions the relevance of the word to Latinas. "With white people, it's more self-conscious, more about the reading. It kind of seems whiny. Strong women figures in Latin culture—la Virgen de Guadalupe, Dolores Huerta—they're fighting for *basic* rights, not feminist rights."

Still, Ale has progressive ideas about women. "I don't believe even a little bit in marriage. It's all about taking care of someone. I never would get married and stop working." And she is dubious about using sex or flirtation to get what you want. "I don't think it's necessary for women to be as cold as steel all the time. But in your workplace, you shouldn't have to compromise."

Both girls immediately mention rape as a central women's issue in their community. "It's amazing the number of people I know that have been raped," Zoe mentions. "And sometimes they don't even think twice about it." Ale agrees, "It's ludicrous how often it happens here. This city has so much turmoil, and it seems like the power struggles are manifested in rape."

ALEJANDRA (TOP); ZOE (BOTTOM)

Isis and Violeta

I leave Elena's house and drive to Cass Café in Detroit's Cultural District. Here I pass galleries and abandoned lots, studios and old train stations—the ultimate industrial/chic. I am meeting up with Isis, twenty-three, and Violeta, twenty-one, both students at Wayne State. Violeta is an undergrad, cheerful and sweet, half–African American and half–Panamanian. Isis is a little more stoic, but speaks wisely and concisely. She is getting her master's degree in bilingual education and is a graduate of Barnard College, which, according to her, makes her "at least a quasifeminist."

Both of the girls are wary of the label, though. "I don't feel well-versed in the subject," Violeta says. "I'm going to school at Wayne State, and I know that that's because women fought for it, but I don't think the word 'feminist' fits." Isis agrees. "I think my being black usually comes before my being a woman. Sometimes it feels like you have to choose." We start on a long tangent about the misogyny in hip-hop, and Isis offers, "That is a perfect example of when I'm torn between being a woman or being black first. If you call out men for being sexist, it's like you're betraying black people in a way." Mostly they feel, as Isis puts it, that "feminism has been presented as a white thing."

ISIS (TOP); VIOLETA (BOTTOM)

> **"My being black usually comes before my being a woman. Sometimes it feels like you have to choose."** —Isis

But what about bell hooks? Angela Davis? Michele Wallace, whom we plan to interview in New York? None of these black women shy away from being called feminists. Isis and Violeta offer their strong opinions about violence and rape and single women raising families alone, and they're so aware and tapped in. So why does feminism still have this white, rich connotation?

"I'm not all that up on the theory," Isis concedes. "I haven't read enough about it." But the two young women seem intrigued. A little while later, via email, Violeta writes to tell me that she recently registered for a Women and Health Disparities class and got involved with Think Girl, a nonprofit that empowers Detroit women. "You've skyrocketed a consciousness in me and I'm starting a habit of acting on it," she writes. Sometimes the core of feminism's meaning is resonant enough to surpass the exclusive history it drags around with it.

Carmen and Sarah

"The coolest, strangest women I've met have come out of this city," says Sarah. "They mean what they say—and they look you in the eye."

Carmen and Sarah have invited me to breakfast at a diner with real gingham tablecloths and an all-steel exterior. Carmen, twenty-one, and Sarah, twenty-four, go to Wayne State with Isis and Violeta. Carmen grew up in "Mexico-town near the bridge" and is taking a class about women and social movements. Sarah is going to school part-time and working a bunch of jobs at once. Carmen and Sarah are both self-proclaimed feminists. Carmen attributes this to growing up in "a household of women, a family run exclusively by my mother," a woman who must have the only immigration law firm on earth that's run out of her own home.

Sarah embraces feminism, too, and she credits

> **"I want to stay in the community, to talk to other women about safety and protecting themselves."** —Carmen

the urge to her five years working at a bike shop, ever since her bike broke and she had no choice but to ask a man to fix it for her. She decided she would learn how to do it herself so that the next time it happened she wouldn't have to go through that bullshit. Both Carmen and Sarah agree that the auto industry brings an extra air of macho to the city, that's it's just that much harder to be respected as a capable woman here. Sarah tells me that men come into the bike shop and are immediately doubtful, giving looks that read, "Are you *sure* you know what you're doing, babe?"

Both women nod vigorously when I ask if they plan to stay in Detroit. "The city brought industrialization to the United States," Carmen sighs. "Now it's a mass exodus because the auto industry is screwed. I want to stay in the community where I was raised, to talk to other women about safety and protecting themselves." The girls insist that Detroit is on the brink of a movement, but Sarah worries about the dual job of raising a family and being an effective community organizer. "You have to put a lot of quality time into both. Men are not socialized to think that way, and that's usually why their issues get pushed first. Women have to work extra hard to be heard."

SARAH (TOP); CARMEN (BOTTOM)

FLINT

Afew months ago, my dad gave a speech at University of Michigan–Flint, where he met Melodee, a twenty-seven-year-old born and bred Flint resident. She was the first woman he thought of when I told him about our plans for *Girldrive*, so I set up an appointment with her after Detroit. After driving for an hour, I reach the outskirts of Flint. The only association I have with the city is the time that I learned about the United Auto Workers' 1937 sit-down strike. Given that Melodee met my dad at a labor conference, I have a feeling that she's absorbed some of that union-bred sense of justice, too.

Melodee and Krystal

Melodee meets me at a diner in Flint with another badass women in tow. Melodee works in Ann Arbor as a documentarian for the Corporation for a Skilled Workforce. She comes from a long line of autoworkers. (My hunch about Melodee is right: "At Thanksgiving, my family thanks God and the union!" she says.) Krystal, who has a degree in Spanish and is pursuing another one in anthropology, had just spent the summer in Venezuela making a documentary about cooperative movements there.

Both answer yes when I ask them whether they are feminists. Melodee calls herself a "born-again feminist." It was a word that turned her off when she was little because her mom was a "black sheep, a pontificator of feminism," a woman who would stand up for herself in public. To Mel, this was

> **"I witnessed my mom go through a lot of chaos and confusion and abuse, and I remember thinking I couldn't be that way."**
>
> —**Krystal**

"totally embarrassing. I thought, *If that's a feminist, I don't want to be one.*" But when she was twenty-three, finishing community college, she met some cool feminists who got her thinking critically about her gender. Krystal is a little more hesitant. "I guess I am, yeah. I witnessed my mom go through a lot of chaos and confusion and abuse, and I remember thinking I couldn't be that way."

But the discussion doesn't end there. We sit in that diner booth for nearly three hours, hashing out the traps and contradictions of modern feminism. "I just want to live in a white picket fence. I still want it even though I don't cognitively buy it," Melodee muses. These women embrace feminist ideas, but not without invoking the challenges posed by pop feminism.

Like Carmen and Sarah, Melodee is dedicated to the area, to reviving the once-bustling industrial city. Mel is perfectly happy being completely broke in Flint as long as she can change the way people are thinking. Krystal disagrees. "I'm definitely getting out of here soon," she assures me. "I feel unwelcome. I have unconventional experiences and thoughts, and sometimes in a city like this, people don't want to hear it."

MELODEE (TOP); KRYSTAL (BOTTOM)

YPSILANTI

By some stroke of luck, Emma comes home in time to join me in Ypsilanti for the last date—with activist and Chicana feminist Martha Cotera. When we arrive at her daughter Maria's house, tired and starved, Maria reads our minds and heats us up a scrumptious feast of vegetarian leftovers. We discover that she is a women's studies professor at the University of Michigan in Ann Arbor. It's obvious that Martha has had no problem passing down feminism to her daughter. Maria's own small daughter is already fast asleep in her bed, and I have a feeling she'll catch on sometime soon, too.

Martha and Maria

Martha spent her early childhood in Mexico and grew up in Texas from the time she was nine. She was raised in a fundamentalist Christian family, but she knew that she didn't want to get married until she graduated college. "So many of my friends got sidetracked," she said. "I felt it was important to survive economically, since it so much affects your dependence on a man."

Martha talks animatedly about her career as a political activist, historian, and teacher, telling us about the founding days of the Raza Unida Party in Texas, the Texas Women's Political Caucus, and the National Women's Political Caucus. She tells us of the stifling tension between white and minority women during the 1970s Women's Liberation Movement. "Chicana feminism was more explicitly about the economic," Martha explains. "We thought that if we joined the movement, we could add our strength and promote issues—like those of migrant/farmer women, working class women." But the groups' agendas often fundamentally clashed. Martha recalls, for instance, the key difference in perspectives about abortion between white and Latina women. "It was all about 'choice.' Abortion was seen as an individual right; the decision was not community-based like it was in Latina families."

"I don't think much has changed," remarks Maria, "What does choice mean? It's presented as the right to have an abortion. True choice would mean living in a state where I'm a high school student, I'm seventeen, I really want to have the baby, and I can have it without having to drop out. Or I'm a welfare mom, and if I have another baby I won't be taken off the rolls. It's framed like you'll be paying for it for the rest of your life." Besides, "The issue of minority women's bodies, the way they've been historically exploited and experimented on, encompasses so much more than abortion."

"That's not only true for women of color," I say. "If a woman lives in a conservative community that doesn't talk about safe sex, she's likely to be misinformed about other sex-related health issues, so the issue of choice is actually too narrow when it comes to where young women need information and education."

Nowadays, Martha runs political workshops for women running for public office. She seems hopeful about young women following in her footsteps, saying, "I never have problems recruiting young women to political campaigns, particularly if the candidate is a woman." But, she adds, these women "don't necessarily call themselves feminists. That's a luxury that we didn't have—to not be put on the spot, to be or not to be." I struggle to interpret Martha's tone. Is she disappointed or proud of our generation? Is she pointing out the mark of progress or the lack of self-awareness? Either way, she seems to think we're doing just fine.

MARTHA AND MARIA

CHAPTER 2

On the Road, Again

THE OPEN ROAD

I press my foot on the gas, heart pounding. We are leaving Chicago, headed west. The steady beat of New Order begins the soundtrack of the movie we have seen a million times, but have never been in. Smiles spread like lightning across our faces. Our road trip has begun. We erase our minds, for a blank slate is the best state. We anticipate strange terrain. Unknown adventures and mishaps will shape every mile. The road tells us what to do. Scream, it says, throw your head out the window at one hundred miles an hour and let the wind whip against your face. Drive fearlessly through pitch black pouring rain, thick Midwestern morning fog. Gaze out the window. Notice the velvet black cows grazing on the ochre cornfields of Nebraska, snow capping the icy blue grand Tetons of Wyoming. Watch the fluorescent glow of fuchsia motel signs click off in the gray dawn, while sipping your complimentary coffee. Pull over to gawk at swirls of evergreen trees dipped in the brightest autumn hues, frosted with Montana mist. Every turn of the car brings a new excuse for dreamers. This is the rush of the road, seeing the highway stretch out endlessly and flipping it the bird. We are tirelessly moving forward and never lagging behind. Make the rules up as you go along. This must be what freedom feels like.

Every moment is fresh and vivid during this initial week on the road. We are opening our sleepy eyes from our world-weary slumber. While the language we used to describe our experiences was sincere, it was entrenched in a cinematic and literary idea of road tripping that we could not separate from own. Cultural amnesia followed us everywhere. "God, this is like that movie!" yet we could never remember the scene. Each philosophical musing was fraught with the stains of past travelers. Life imitated art in the most curious blend.

The American road trip is a charged symbol that we are taught to recognize from a young age. Whether it is the rebellious soul-searching of *On the Road* and *Thelma and Louise,* the colonial adventures of the Oregon Trail computer game or the capitalist dream of the Gold Rush, we have been trained to view road travel as an inherently American activity. Its inspirational power seems to penetrate every aspect of cultural production and collective memory. We think of '50s convertibles at the drive-in and James Dean's deadly game of chicken. There are the '60s VW vans following the Dead and covered in flower power, materialistic teenagers in the '80s obsessed with a red Corvette as the key to an independence located in trips to the mall or make-out lane. From the dysfunctional family trip to the Grand Canyon ("are we there yet?") to the proliferation of RV culture, we are a nation obsessed with vehicular myth.

—*Emma*

Note: The full text for this piece can be read in the Postscript on page 212.

DRIVING WEST

Emma is back from New York, and we are leaving Chicago—for real now— headed west. The car is crammed out the ears with anything we would ever need to survive a road trip. I drive first, and about an hour into the trip I glance over at Emma, who is looking out the window. Gone are the worry lines and tears that have marred her face this past week. I am relieved and happy that our first day consists of pure driving. On this thirteen-hour stretch, we have plenty of time to break the ice with our new companion—the road.

JACKSON HOLE

We drive hours and hours straight, from the mustardy landscape of Nebraska to Yellowstone National Park's gateway, Jackson Hole. Suddenly, the autumn weather we had left behind turns wintry. We enter a Tim Burton–esque pine-tree wonderland, where the sideways snow hitting our windshield reminds us of that screensaver where stars ambush your vision. We are not even sure we are going the right way, but we finally arrive on Shelby's doorstep at 11:00 PM stupid-tired and ready for a massage.

Shelby

Shelby grew up right in Jackson Hole, and has been living at her mom's since she graduated college this past June. The discussion begins with the character of Wyoming in general, since Emma's and my ignorance of the state is painfully obvious. "It's the 'equality state,' the first state to grant women's suffrage," Shelby tells us. But she makes sure we know that the macho Wyoming cowboy myth often rings true here, that men who "drive trucks, shoot guns, and marry women for the cooking" abound. These are the men who label women "feminazis" if they simply speak their mind.

Nonetheless, Shelby assures us that there are Wyoming women who defiantly reject this machismo. She has long considered herself a feminist, which to her means, among other things, being sexually empowered. Her first feminist hero was Veronica Franco, the sixteenth-century Venetian courtesan and poet who used her powers of seduction to do the forbidden—become literate. Shelby acknowledges that while women have always used their sexual power to advance, there is fine line between empowering and degrading.

SHELBY

> **"Right now I** don't give a fuck— **I want to explore."**
>
> —Shelby

In fact, her number one concern as a feminist is girls' obsession with appearance, and the general toxicity of girl culture.

Tomorrow she is moving to San Diego without a job or a plan. Her overeducated friends from college are already climbing the ranks in their entry-level jobs, but she has no desire to rush into the rat race. She tells us that her relaxed attitude comes from her slower-paced hometown and the monetary benefits of living in what she calls "the Beverly Hills of Wyoming." Shelby quips, "I can buy pretty leather furniture later. Right now I don't give a fuck—I want to explore." Emma and I understand. Having time to explore and not falling victim to postgrad pressures is what motivated us to take this trip in the first place. To us, feminism is hopelessly intertwined with figuring out who you are and what you truly want.

SIÓUX FALLS

It takes us another two days to drive to Sioux Falls, where we only have time to stay for a night before we go to Lake Andes in western South Dakota for an interview. We scoop up our friend Antonia from the Sioux Falls airport—she's joining us for our Dakotas stretch—and we head to a bar one of our friends recommended. We order some drinks, eager to fill Antonia in on our adventures thus far.

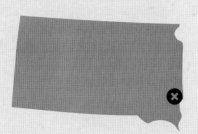

THE TOP HAT

T he Top Hat is divey and dirt-cheap, a bar filled with young people on a Friday night. Since the mixed drinks are $2.50, we have no problem sucking a few down. We strike up a conversation with a chatty brunette. We ask her one question, since we don't have a full hour to talk: "What's the number one thing on your mind lately?"

She immediately answers: single motherhood. "I'm a twenty-seven-year-old bartender with a six-year-old daughter," she slurs. "There's no one helping me. I'm on welfare, but they don't factor in what it takes to live. You think that people on welfare are lazy bums, but I work my ass off, and I can still barely pay my daughter's insurance premiums." She tells us she's a few credits shy of getting a master's, but she has no time to do work without help. "Does a degree in anthropology count anywhere? Fuck no!" she blurts emotionally. "I'd rather be a bartender making cash."

Bartending sucks, too, though, she promises. "You're a vagina behind the bar," she says. "You're not a real person to most people." She apologizes for being so forward—"I just have a lot of things on my mind." "Hey, we asked!" I reassure her. We never do catch her name, but Emma manages to snap a few shots of her with Antonia, deep in conversation.

ANTONIA (LEFT) AND OUR NEW FRIEND

LAKE ANDES

We set out for an interview in Lake Andes, a town a hundred miles southwest of Sioux Falls that lies in the boundaries of the Yankton Sioux reservation. The drive there offers stark, never-ending stretches of abandoned farmland dotted with larger-than-life trees. Soon we enter the town, a place that feels like it hasn't changed in forty years. Besides Main Street, there is no semblance of hustle-and-bustle, only curling ivy, chipping paint, and rusty bicycles. It seems an unlikely host to the nation's first reservation-based women's resource center for Native American women, but we prepare to keep our ears open as we step inside.

Charon and Natalie

Here we were, in front of probably the most visible advocate for Native American women in the country, and the first thing Charon Asetoyer tells us is: "Traditionally, native women are not feminists."

Charon explains, "The women of my tribe always had the right to vote, to have a say in the traditional governance. We were landowners, we had the right to determine the size of our family." The way she sees it, native women in contemporary society are "trying to maintain rights rather than acquire them." Born into the Comanche tribe in Oklahoma, and married into the Yankton Sioux in Lake Andes, Charon has been an ardent activist for native rights since the '60s. She founded the Native American Women's Health Education Resource Center in 1988, and still works as the executive director. The center tackles a huge range of issues—everything from domestic violence to AIDS prevention—and funds shelters, education programs, radio broadcasting, and food pantries.

"So feminism isn't useful at all to the Native American community?" I ask. "That's a very abstract question," Charon points out. "Feminism isn't a tool, it's a state of mind—that you are equal to everyone else. It's a legal presence, something that women are entitled to. Some women accept their social status in an oppressive society. I think a feminist is someone who doesn't accept that oppression."

Charon makes it clear that the center is bigger than exclusively women's issues. "The biggest challenge [for native women] is racism, which is probably a much bigger set of issues than the feminist issues. Most of the oppression felt by the native culture is land-based. The colonization has gotten a little more civilized, but it has never stopped."

Charon is confident about the activism of young people in the native community. Perhaps as a hint to us, she tells us that the young interns coming from fancy schools get quite an education. "Their minds are blown by these layers and layers of legal battles. Go talk to Natalie over there."

So we go talk to her. Natalie, twenty-one, is from Denver and has come from Hampshire College to intern for a semester in Lake Andes. She is working on a report for the Center about the lack of Plan B in emergency rooms for assault victims. At night she works at the domestic violence shelter down the street. Natalie was "getting lost in academia" and wanted to get back on the ground. She relates to feminism. "I grew up in a rough neighborhood, and having gone through some of these issues we're fighting for right now, it really touches on me and my body."

NATALIE (TOP); CHARON (BOTTOM)

FARGO

Fargo couldn't be more different from the dilapidated beauty of rural South Dakota. We are greeted by stretches of strip malls, fast food restaurants, and rows of houses built by the same manufacturer. It is Sunday, and the smaller businesses are closed; the entire city is quiet. The huge sky is all the same muted gray color. Our first order of business is a chat with three women who work with the only abortion clinic in North Dakota.

Red River Ladies

Less than twenty-four hours after we contacted Tammi Kromenaker, the director of the Red River Women's Clinic in Fargo, we had three interviewees eager to tell what it was like to work at the only abortion clinic in North Dakota. A far cry from New York City, where there's a Planned Parenthood in every borough, the Dakotas have been positioned in the media as a critical, precipitous region where abortion battles play out.

Becca, twenty-two, started at the clinic two years ago working at the front desk; Emily, twenty-four, and Dena Marie, twenty-three, are both volunteer escorts—that is, they accompany women entering the clinic for an abortion and shelter them from the angry and often violent protestors. All consider themselves feminists. We're dying to know how people react to their involvement with Red River—and to their self-proclaimed feminism for that matter. All three women share a look when we ask.

"My father is a minister," Emily offers, "so it's not something that we've openly talked about. But my parents are interested in what I'm doing. There are times when we shake our heads at each other, but there are times when we support each other too."

Dena Marie and Becca aren't so lucky. When Dena Marie was on television protesting the pro-life campaign 40 Days for Life, she tells us, "My grandmother was devastated and told my dad she was going to be praying for a long time." Becca laughs and tells us that her mom begged her to keep her job a secret from her dad. "In my family it's very hush hush, like, 'That's Becca, she works at a clinic, she likes abortions, she's gay—just don't bring it up.'" Emily adds, "There are some people I will tell and others I won't. But still there's this stigma of 'What are you doing there? Which side are you on?'"

I pose a hard question: Can one be a Christian and be pro-choice?

Emily says yes. "I was raised Lutheran, and for me it's more about caring for the person and showing love. Jesus himself hung out with prostitutes. It's most important that I reach out to people who are struggling and help them in whatever way they choose for themselves."

Dena agrees, saying that one of the coolest people she knows is a pastor who spoke about her own decision to have an abortion. But Becca shakes her head adamantly. "All of the anti-choice people outside of the clinic are all connected with religion, and it makes me really wary of what religion provides for people. It seems like a trap of brainwashing. But I'd like to see our patients get support from their own religion, at least."

Another question comes to mind: "Can you be pro-life and be a feminist?" A few days earlier,

FROM LEFT: DENA, EMILY, BECCA

I had Googled Feminists for Life and discovered that they're one of the most radical pro-life organizations out there. Can "feminist" really be interpreted however one wants?

"I have a friend who is a pro-life feminist," Dena says. "We've agreed that she can be both as long as she pushes the common ground, which is preventing unwanted pregnancy." Emily responds, "Yes, you have to be in favor of good sex education. That means talking about sex and what it's about—intimacy and relationships and consequences and STDs. It has to be done on a public level, in schools."

Again, Becca shakes her head. "To me, the two can't mesh. A woman who says, 'I'm pro-life, but I believe in choice' is elevating what her choice is. Shaming women, however subtly, is not what the pro-choice movement is all about."

Beth

Beth invites us to the farm she grew up on in Moorhead, North Dakota, a couple miles east of Fargo. We sit around the table in her family's storybooklike farmhouse, restored after "it was appraised at zero," she tells us. Beth is living with her parents while she attends Bible college up the road at Fargo Baptist Church, where her dad is a pastor. "God is definitely a big part of my life," she says. Beth is also a budding photographer, who works corporately and started her own company,

BETH

Eden Photography, about a year ago.

Bright-eyed and chipper, twenty-year-old Beth tells us she is not a feminist. "I don't believe that women should be doormats—we're all equal to God—but God gives us different roles," she explains. "If this is his will, for women to raise the next generation, a woman's going to be her happiest raising children." "But what about your flourishing photography career?" I ask. "Are you going to give that up to be a mother?"

"No," she replies. "You can have your business on the side, as sort of a 'fallback,' but your focus should be on your family and God."

Beth associates the term feminism with what it means in "the career world," and in that sense she believes in equal rights for both genders. She clarifies, "I don't think that certain people shouldn't get a job because they're a woman, but I do think in a marriage, you should submit. There are definitely roles for a husband and wife, and feminism would be erasing that."

I wonder if Beth sees her religion or ideas about gender roles as part of a bigger political message about American women.

"Not really," she replies. "I try to do my best, but I'm not too worried about politics. God's got it in control."

THE FARM

We are three city girls in a playground . . .

The fall colors are so rich, the field so remote . . .

Antonia perches herself next to a white picket fence . . .

No wonder Beth's optimism isn't marred by the outside world!

PRARIE ROSE

Prairie Rose

In the early evening we meet with Prairie Rose at her apartment. She is the last interviewee in a jam-packed, raw Fargo day. She is a member of the Berthold Reservation in northwest North Dakota, and was born in Fargo to a German-Russian mother and an extremely devout Cheyenne Arikara father. She now works with a local promoter, but her "heart and passion really lies with social justice issues," particularly those affecting the Native American population. Prairie Rose is already the chair of the Human Relations Commission in Fargo, and the city of Fargo liaison to the Native American Commission.

Prairie Rose, twenty-eight, describes herself as a feminist, but reminds us (like Charon did) that the word sounds a little strange in the context of her culture. "I understand it more as humanism," she says. "Most Native Americans are not educated in the language of feminism." She explains the relationship between the sexes as a "trade-off." "The Western interpretation of native culture is that women were very domesticated," she explains. "But with this comes a lot of balance . . .

the women were the backbone of our society. The men protected us. Women were responsible for education. We were the healers, the doctors, the midwives, we had power. The culture was compassionate and equitable."

A breath after recounting this symbiotic history, Prairie Rose tells us that Native American women suffer two or three times the rate of domestic violence, rape, and incest of their Caucasian counterparts. Prairie Rose herself had an abusive father who suffered from alcoholism. "Traditionally, native women would not need this concept of 'feminism.' But our way of life was taken away from us. When you are a people who has lost everything, who has been relocated, who has been forced into this whole assimilation process, you lose yourselves—because of oppression we became the oppressors."

Like Charon, Prairie Rose sees a new generation of women trying to reinvent this delicate balance, to bring back "the values that held us up so high as people." But, she tells us, "it's a hard cycle to break."

CHAPTER 3 **When It Rains, It Pours**

SEATTLE

The instant we reach Seattle, it starts raining steadily. We settle in at a wine bar just outside the city to wait for our first interviewee, Carla DeSantis. There is a lull in Seattle—it's a beautiful collection of hills but has an unnerving serenity that would later be described to us as the "Seattle Freeze." With the rainwater seeping into our jeans just from the quick run from the car into the bar, we catch up on some emails as we prepare to delve into our first major U.S. city together.

Carla

In steps Carla, founder and editor of *ROCK-RGRL* Magazine and a women-in-rock advocate. Emma is piping with fan girl excitement for the interview—Carla is on a first-name basis with many of her childhood music idols. A longtime feminist, she got into the Northwest women's music scene when she was thirty-six and going through a divorce. "The angry music was very soothing," she tells us. Soon after she founded

> *"I hope women will have a place in rock that's not just a sexy picture licking the neck of a guitar."* —Carla

ROCKRGRL, a magazine that covers women in rock that started as a sixteen-page xeroxed zine, she quit her job to focus her attention on publishing it full-time.

She tells us that the biggest obstacle she's seen to feminism in the music scene has been the infighting that happened in the early '90s. Women like Courtney Love, Kathleen Hanna, and Sarah McLachlan were at odds, splitting hairs to the point that they couldn't appreciate each other. "It was cliquey—they never learned how to work together," she says. Part of what Carla tried to do with *ROCKRGRL* was bring these different groups together and highlight the value of each. But some biggies—like Juliana Hatfield and L7—didn't want to be interviewed for the zine because they didn't want to be primarily identified as feminist.

Emma muses whether it's possible, in a world full of Avrils and Ashlees, for the country to embrace a rebellious, punky, feminist musician "that's not Pink." Carla is skeptical. "Britney doesn't even write her own music. That's not a role model—that's Barbie." But she adds that there's always something new—and that she hopes that women will have a place in rock that's not "just in a sexy picture licking the neck of a guitar."

CARLA

BANJI (TOP); GINA (BOTTOM)

Gina and Banji

We rush to meet Gina at Cha Cha, a red-tinted hipster bar in the Capitol Hill area. Gina is a twentysomething musician who recently abandoned her folky, Ani DiFranco style to become one-half of Team Gina, a queer hip-hop duo. She is an old friend of Emma's from her Riot Grrrl days, an older sister figure who, like Emma, first found feminism through that movement.

Banji, one of Gina's friends and a Seattle native, joins her on the interview. She points to Gina and informs us, "I know so many awesome women in this city, and Gina is the only one I know who is a feminist." Wait, what? Even in Seattle, the liberal, open-minded, grungy mecca? "Yes," Banji says. "Seattle is so equal for everybody that individual groups get lost."

Gina was relieved when Emma wrote her about *Girldrive* and was glad to hear Emma was still "feminist-identified." Originally from DC, Gina moved to Seattle a couple years back after living in New York for a period of time. She realized relatively quickly that both the female rock and lesbian communities were surprisingly apoliticized here. "Seattle is so nice and calm," she says. "You don't get bothered and cat-called on the street like you do in New York. That's what made me a feminist in the first place—getting angry that this happened to me every day." She tells us about the gay scene in Seattle, saying that

"I'm not a feminist, I'm a person."
—Banji

the girls are "cute, nonaggressive, fashiony." We get the impression that Seattle overall is passive, overwhelmingly white, and not at all angry.

When I ask Banji whether she considers herself a feminist, she says, "No, I consider myself a pyramidist." A what? She tells us that feminism is thinking too small, that we should start at the top of the problem rather than being concerned with an isolated part of civilization. Gina is unconvinced, and so am I. "Identity politics can be fucked up," I say, "but isn't it a little paralyzing to tackle every problem on earth?" Banji persists. "I'm not a feminist, I'm a person." But Gina sees the value in separatism. We need to "rally around the point of oppression without the oppressor in the room," she concludes.

STARTING SOMEWHERE

We talk for a while at the bar with Gina, Banji, and a few of their friends about the term "humanist." That term has always pissed me off. I mean, aren't we all humanists? Of course your heart can bleed for everybody. It should. Of course everything is connected and one major problem like sexism can't be overcome without taking on racism, classism, and every other –ism. But come on. To dodge the word "feminist" and say you're a humanist seems like a cop-out. After all, isn't it just a term that covers the bases of being a good person but doesn't obligate you to take any sort of action? Even if self-proclaimed humanists are politically active, they are still, in a way, refusing to align themselves with a more explicit cause. Fighting for everyone all at once leaves us at a standstill, and you have to start somewhere.

—Nona

Colleen

The next morning, we walk to breakfast with Colleen, twenty-three, who is the first in her immediate family to move away from the Midwest. She randomly moved to Seattle two months ago with no job, money, or apartment. While still in college, Colleen had a brush with domesticity when her boyfriend, who was going to med school at Duke and bought a house with the intention of having Colleen move in with him. Ultimately, he realized she wasn't ready and they broke up—just like that.

Before we meet Colleen, Emma had described her as a bundle of contradictions. Colleen was a fellow art major with Emma at University of Chicago, but they never hung out. Defying the hipster norm of the art department and of University of Chicago in general, Colleen was committed to her sorority. She is blond with a sunny disposition, yet for her senior show she produced a series of brooding nude self-portraits. When we ask about the apparent contradiction between sororities and feminism, she describes her experience as "the most feminist, girl-power thing I've ever done." (She professes that a UChicago sorority tends to be more cerebral than a state school's.) She says that if feminism includes forming meaningful female relationships, then she is a "personal feminist"—but feels detached from the political activism of feminism.

Colleen tells us that her sisters were confused by her paintings but were still very supportive. "What was the deal with those, anyway?" Emma asks. "Your work always seemed pretty feminist to me." In a surprising moment, Colleen tells us the impetus for the portraits: A few years ago, she passed out in the shower, split her head open, and was taken completely naked to the hospital. When she awoke, she learned that one of her friends had committed suicide. She has been obsessed with mortality and the fragility of her body ever since. Emma was shocked. "Why didn't you ever say anything about that in critiques?" she asks. Colleen says she was doing the art partly for personal catharsis, and admits that she never felt comfortable with the art faculty. "My sorority sisters knew more about my art than my advisers did," she says. "I felt like they could understand better."

COLLEEN; ONE OF COLLEEN'S PAINTINGS (TOP RIGHT)

PÓRTLAND

We receive a warm welcome from our old camp friend Danya (a.k.a. Chocolate, a childhood nickname that has never quite been explained). She lives in a huge, hippyish, ramshackle house, complete with a sewing room and a pizza pantry. We got in late, but we still have the urge to explore a bit before our succession of appointments the next day. A couple hours earlier, Emma's friend Sam had sent her an enigmatic text that included a Portland address and the message: "Don't ask what it is. Just go." These instructions lead us to a bar in a looming, industrial part of the city where a noise show is going on. The drone of the instruments sets the scene of Portland—alternative, unassuming, and muted by the constant dampness of the Northwest coast.

Andi

The next morning we interview our first Third Wave feminist, Andi Zeisler, cofounder and editor of *Bitch* magazine. Andi's formative years were much like ours—she grew up in New York City, went to a prestigious high school, and was raised by liberal Jews. She first became a feminist at a young age, nine or ten: "I remember thinking, *This is bullshit,* but I didn't have a word for it yet." Her agitation took her from Colorado College to San Francisco, where she and her roommate, Lisa Jervis, first hatched the idea of *Bitch.* "It initially started because we were frustrated readers." They decided to develop a space to critically discuss and appreciate the simultaneously "poisonous and pleasurable" aspects of pop culture.

Does being the editor of a "feminist" magazine make her feel responsible for countering the low-self-esteem machine of mainstream women's magazines?

"I think of *Bitch* as part of a progressive media diet, but it can't provide it all," she says. "We feel a responsibility to call that stuff out, but most women who pick up a magazine named 'Bitch' will be aware of it."

However, there has been much resistance to the name "Bitch." Even Andi's mom worried she may come off as too stern, claiming there is a "difference between strident and nice feminism." But *Bitch*'s appeal is its unwillingness to sit quietly for fear of being labeled ugly or (eek!) bitchy. Andi notes that for every criticism they get, they receive equally appreciative letters, even from Second Wavers. But while reclaiming sexist terms was an important aspect of the Third Wave, she acknowledges that its championing of individual choice has had its negative consequences. "If you're a feminist and a stripper, and the guys watching you don't know that, does it really matter?"

She understands our generation's uneasiness with the term "feminism" itself, blaming it in part on "the conservative noise machine that gets louder every year—people who equate feminism with man-hating and castration." But she thinks coming up with a new term is silly: "It's the concept of women's equality that people have a problem with, so whatever word we come up with is going to be turned into a bad one."

—**Emma**

Sprinavasa

After a couple hours in a classic Northwest café, Emma and I walk up to Sprinavasa's apartment on the east side. She went to Oberlin College and was raised in northeast Portland, which had traditionally been a mostly black neighborhood, but has seen a recent influx of "hippies and hipsters." Sprina (as she calls herself) was raised by her mother, a machinist for Freightliner and one of the few women—out of over three thousand employees—who work on the machines. She worked all the time so that she could send Sprina to a prestigious, mostly white private school.

Sprina worked a couple of summers at Freightliner, too. She now works at the front desk at the Hilton downtown and has been planning to open a jewelry boutique with her friend for the past several months. Has she experienced sexism as an entrepreneur or a machinist? "Not really," she says. Sprina knows there's still a lot of sexism in this country, but she claims not to have personally experienced much of it.

She reconsiders when we ask her about her personal relationships. "Actually, yes, now that you say it," she concedes. "Being a smart, outspoken woman, when you approach a dude like that they get intimidated." After Oberlin, she came back to Portland and had trouble relating to men her age. "I don't have much connection with men here, especially men of color, because there aren't that many here who are educated. Or, I have a guy friend who is going to college, but just to get a job that pays more money." With her female friends, it's different. "I'm naturally just closer to women," she says, "but I love going to school. I don't want to have to dumb myself down for the purpose of dating."

Emma wonders aloud whether feminism came up in Sprina's household, since she was raised by a single mother who worked at a traditionally male job. "I always saw my mother as an image of a strong woman who stood on her own two feet," Sprina says, "but I first learned about feminism in school." Even then, "I never really got a good sense of it. My first impression was that it was an angry white woman thing. After that, the only feminist women of color I met were lesbian or bisexual. So I thought, 'I'm for women, but I just don't fit in.'" Sprina thinks she considers herself a feminist, but that she "has created her own definition within it." She also thinks it's possible for all women to work together: "Race separates people less than it once did," she asserts.

SPRINAVASA

gigi!

if you are bored when you're alone, it's your own fault.

ENDLESS, NAMELESS

I have always glamorized the Northwest from afar as a grunge mecca of laid-back cool. I imagined Portland and Seattle as a lazy afternoon filled with cute boys in flannel shirts drinking local coffee on porches, playing indie rock in basements. Nearby is Olympia, Washington, home to Riot Grrrl, and when we passed Sleater-Kinney Road en route to Seattle, my heart leaped imagining the dark, rainy, England-away-from-England vibe mixing with the Pacific breeze and guitar riffs.

I was surprised to find that Seattle is supercutesy, almost claustrophobically so. The people are really crunchy, but the whole place seems squeaky clean. It has edge, but it is cookie-cutter edge. Portland seems equally safe, full of mild-mannered hippies and sleepy cafés.

Still, when we were walking down the polished streets of the indie, queer neighborhood of Capitol Hill in Seattle, I could envision Kurt Cobain pacing down these streets, high on dope and soggy from the rain. I got the same eerie feeling as we trolled the streets of Portland, scoping out the dives and dudes. Despite the packaged bohemia that is no doubt the result of gentrification, there is still a raw, romantic quality to these Northwest cities. The gray sky bathes everything in stillness; the ocean rolls on next door. I want a cup of black coffee. —Emma

CHAPTER 4 — **California Girls** ➡

THE BAY

Our first night in Cali is spent in a mansion in the Oakland Hills, courtesy of my college friend Vanessa who is staying with a famous photographer for a month until she gets settled in San Francisco. As we climb higher and higher over the Bay, we notice an obtrusive U-Haul parked directly below our digs for the night. We park on a drastic slant, giving us the feeling of sliding off into the glittering lights of the valley below. As we settle for the night, Vanessa explains that this week has been kinda crazy—the house was being rented for thousands of dollars a day to a film crew working on a commercial. Emma and I crack up and give each other a knowing look: We have officially landed in California.

Rebecca and Jane

Our New York City buddy, Marianna, is meeting up with us for our California journey, and we take her to interview a mother-daughter pair: Jane, who founded and runs a porn production company called Pantymistress for men with fetishes, and her daughter Rebecca, a twenty-three-year-old feminist who graduated from Wesleyan last year and wrote her honors thesis about the feminist economic potential of the porn industry.

Jane was a magazine editor and started Pantymistress in 1993 after dating a lingerie fetishist. "I thought it was very creative, but he felt so much shame and guilt around his sexuality. I figured other men must feel that way, so I started creating audio fantasies for them." The company took

off, and eventually she was running Pantymistress full-time. Is she a feminist? Not in the conventional sense. "I might be considered a feminist because I started a business and am sex-positive, but I personally have never used the term." Her contribution, she says, is to de-shame fantasies. "Fantasies pick us; we don't pick our fantasies," she tells us.

Rebecca grew up helping her mom package tapes for the customers, never listening to the fantasies but gradually understanding porn's possibility for women's economic empowerment. "The porn industry exists to make money, period. They don't think about feminism." But she notes that this profitable industry has a space for women stars and CEOs. "I often compare Jenna Jameson to Oprah and Martha Stewart. She's created an empire, and now she doesn't even have to be in movies," Rebecca says.

Rebecca thinks the opportunity in porn exists on the consumer side, as well. She says there is a market for feminist porn, not because it says "feminist" on the box, but because people think it's hot when the porn actress enjoys herself. "People get confused when I say 'feminist porn,' so I've stopped saying it. People start to think soft-focus, romantic, making love. It looks exactly like any porn you would see, except that the woman is having a good time. It's porn that respects the experience of women."

> **"Feminist porn looks exactly like any porn you would see, except that the woman is having a good time."**
> —Rebecca

REBECCA (TOP); JANE (BOTTOM)

Carey

In the afternoon we meet up with Carey Perloff, who came of age in the Second Wave and runs the American Conservatory Theater in downtown San Francisco. She tells us right off the bat about her concern over the rise in the number of stay-at-home moms. I remind her that many young women don't feel that dads and the culture are ready to split the work with them. She agrees that society needs to make structural changes but says that women shouldn't just "give up. Why are we granting all these scholarships to women if they're not even going to use their education?"

But what about education for its own sake, or women who don't define success by their careers? (A mother I know pops into my head. She took five years off from work to raise her young kids and now has a job to pay the bills, but defines her personal success not only by her children but by being an Olympic sailor and a politician within her local community.) Carey answers, "It's an upper middle class thing to decide not to work. The woman at the dry cleaners I see every day can't choose to stay home. So what are we [middle class white women] complaining about?"

Jerlina

Jerlina lives in a true Berkeley commune. Technically a co-op, but a commune all the same. A friendly hippie leads us from the sprawling courtyard into a colorful wooden house and up the winding stairs to meet Jerlina. She takes us outside to the garden, where a topless girl in cutoff jean shorts is planting seeds in the afternoon sun.

Jerlina is a twenty-five-year-old student at UC Berkeley getting her PhD in African Diaspora Studies. She tells us about a radical ecofeminist group she just joined. She connects ecofeminism (a movement that unites environmentalism and feminism) to Buddhism, a religion that sees the interconnectedness of all the world's elements. Jerlina was raised with the Buddhist idea of practicing nonviolence and a respect for life, which in turn translates into a respect "for the environment, for water, for women, for everything." She acknowledges that there aren't many women of color in the local ecofeminism movement, but that some of the most famous ecofeminists in the world are from Asian and African countries (like Vandana Shiva, who's from India).

Jerlina is one of the most optimistic women we've heard so far when it comes to her feelings about the future. "There are many women who I want to tell, 'Stand up for yourself!' But I am surrounded by so many powerful, inspirational women that it balances it out." The New Yorker

JERLINA (TOP); CAREY (BOTTOM)

in me is often skeptical of peace-and-positivist Berkeley, but at this moment, Jerlina's hopefulness is nice to hear.

Starhawk

Fresh from Jerlina, we are bubbling with anticipation to meet another ecofeminist—Starhawk, who's a practicing witch and a well-known spokeswoman for pagan and Wiccan ideas. She lives in a purple-and-yellow-painted Victorian, shared communally, stickered with antiwar paraphernalia and brimming inside with stacks of books and boxes of tea. Upstairs is the ritual room, where Starhawk runs weekly Wicca meetings. It is bright and cozy, filled with different objects ranging from drums to votives to goddess statues. Starhawk herself emanates worldly wisdom and an innate kindness that must come from her spiritual openness to the earth and other beings.

She first became involved in feminism in the 1970s, when she joined consciousness raising groups. She soon found that her values best fit with ecofeminism, a movement that believes in a more "intuitive" and spiritual connection between women, nature, and politics. It was at that same time when Starhawk found Wicca and paganism and began to see the connection between goddess-centered religions and an inherent feminine power, an ethos that she believes society has lost through the dominance of patriarchal religions. Starhawk

sees the rhetoric and violence of war being directly linked to the phallocentric nature of religion. "Religion shapes our cultural consciousness," she says. "If god equals male, male is going to equal god. There is an entire history of woman in spirituality that has been suppressed and hidden."

—**Emma**

Bea

Bea is a barrage of striking contrasts—she has a sweet singsong voice; a strong, solid body; a stare that radiates both kindness and steeliness. She is from Decatur, Georgia, but felt drawn to Oakland because it is so "ethnically and linguistically integrated—a place with a lot of community organizing and unity." She works at a library, teaches at a local elementary school, and volunteers at a queer black youth center.

Although she went to public school and grew up in black neighborhoods in the South, her first exposure to feminism was from white, educated lesbians who worked with her in an Atlanta bookstore when she was fifteen. Bea felt like a feminist "more back in the day than now." She identified most with the term when she was coming out as queer in high school.

Feminism is not the direction she sees herself going—she is trying to be more "gender-revolutionary." She explains, "I love women, I'm queer, but being in a lot of women-only spaces in the

BEA (TOP); STARHAWK (BOTTOM)

past, it was a feeling of pro-woman without speaking to masculine women or feminine men." She thinks that feminism still doesn't quite know how to handle the trans community or the continuum of gender.

At the center of Bea's activist impulse is her desire to combat violence. It's the goal of INCITE!, an organization of women of color against violence that she's a part of. She says if she could get behind a "new kind of feminism," she would like it to be framed in terms of "the war and the militarism" that's ingrained in American culture.

Emma says that if there were to be a grassroots women's movement, it would have to "recognize the totality and subtlety of women's experiences." I find myself thinking that maybe *The Vagina Monologues* had it right. Violence is an issue that cuts across class, race, and national lines, whether it's rape, domestic violence, or, as Bea puts it, "women forcing themselves into skinny bodies."

Betita

Elizabeth "Betita" Martinez is a Chicana feminist and a veteran community organizer, writer, and teacher originally

> "My first experience with feminism was with white women, and they didn't seem to see anything to fight against except men." —Betita

from Washington, DC. I pay a quick visit to her house in the Mission while Emma picks the brain of a radical video artist in the Haight. By the time Betita gets through all eighty-three years of her life, we barely have time to talk about young feminists, but she does tell me this: "My first experience with feminism was with white women, and they didn't seem to see anything to fight against except men. I remember going to a meeting with the New York Radical Women on the night that Martin Luther King Jr. was assassinated, and nobody mentioned it! How could you ignore a thing like that? Feminists nowadays tend to be more broadly politicized; they see the connections between gender, race, and class. Not that I'm too critical of those earlier feminists. They were just breaking the ice."

FeMiNiSM & AcADEMIA

On our second night in San Francisco, we meet with four graduates of a small liberal art college in Massachusetts—a nanny, an animal rights activist, an artist-photographer, and a scholar of gender studies. All are opinionated and versed in feminism. But strangely, the interview isn't a success. Our basic questions, like "Do you consider yourself a feminist?" or "How do you see your life through the eyes of a woman?" are met with unbridled suspicion. Our skins crawl with discomfort. The answers to our questions go something like this: "I feel like that question is problematic." Or "That question is too generalizing." We struggle to move on.

These young women are clearly smart, assertive, and passionate. Each of them knows more about the Women's Movement than anyone we've met thus far. But they can't level with us as peers.

Emma's and my relationship to academic feminism has always been love-hate. We realize its power, but we've also noticed how academic feminism alienates young women from concepts they would otherwise be down with.

Many young women, including me, feel that academia often sequesters feminism into a humorless, dry corner of the ivory tower. Even though I have my own favorite feminist theorists, my everyday experience is what fuels my feminism.

Then there's Emma—if anyone could find meaning in academic language, it's her. She always insists that the academic can be personal, which is exactly what's missing from this interview. The girls' answers are riddled with countless disclaimers; they want to make sure they aren't essentializing or generalizing. That means they don't share details of their own lives—getting dressed in the morning, interacting with their bosses, reading the paper—that are disclaimer-free. They're making sure their answers are being fair to all the feminist theory they've ever absorbed.

The problem, we realize, has partly to do with the structure of *Girldrive* itself. This project is, above all, about individual stories and human connections. But we've also been asking our subjects to coexist with preconceived notions of feminist thought. We find out, right here, that asking about "feminism" can only get us so far in our journey. Some women simply won't be familiar enough with the concepts to connect the word to their experience, and some will be, well, too familiar. All we want is a conversation. And if academic feminism really has become so removed from personal experience that it's caused emotional paralysis, then we are determined to change that.

—Nona

SANTA CRUZ

Liana, an old friend of a friend, gives us one of the warmest welcomes possible, taking us out for sushi the moment we arrive in Santa Cruz. Liana tells us that she and her boyfriend are engaged, then shows us the gleaming ring. Twenty-three isn't crazy young to be engaged, but somehow it catches me off guard—are lots of educated, career-driven women with independent spirits getting married so young? I make a mental note to ask Liana about it in our interview. For now, though, we catch up for a couple of hours amid tons of artful, seaside sushi.

Liana

Liana walks us to New Brighton beach for the interview, settling herself on the sand in the late afternoon sun. She went to UC Santa Cruz, initially worked full-time at a health clinic and is now teaching and studying for her education degree. She's half–Cuban, half–Mexican; half–Californian, half–New Yorker.

Liana says, "I never questioned whether I was a feminist," and says that when she was growing up, "Women tied the family together." Liana tells us about her own relationship and her plans to get married and start a family within the next few years, a move she sees in complete accordance with feminism. "I see being a wife and mother as the ultimate chance to be a role model for young women." Emma and I share a glance. I have often expressed to Emma that the landscape of feminism would look quite different today if more Second Wavers had had children. Both our mothers were

exceptions to the rule, having children despite the huge pressure at that point in the movement to focus on career. Our mothers, after all, are our first and most enduring female influence.

Liana touches on her sense of responsibility to young women through teaching and talks about wanting to give the Latino kids in the community a strong female example. "That's why I hesitate to change my name when I get married," she says. "I never thought I would want to change my name growing up until I met Bobby. I take pride in his name and his family, but I have these inner pangs to keep Gomez and let my students know I'm half–Mexican."

> **"I see being a wife and mother as the ultimate chance to be a role model for young women."** —Liana

LIANA

LÓS ANGELES

Óur first introduction to Los Angeles is Venice Beach at night. Julia, who's never met us, has invited the three of us—Emma, Marianna, and I—to stay, even though her sick dog has just come home from the hospital. We are beat, and we end up curling up on the couch and choosing *Pretty Woman* from our huge collection of DVDs. "My mom produced this!" Julia tells us. She divulges a fun fact: "My mother fought to have the last line in the movie, where Julia Roberts tells Richard Gere that she is going to 'rescue him right back.' *Pretty Woman* is not the most feminist movie in the world, but think about it: Without that line, it'd be garbage."

Julia B., Julia G., and Anna

Before we visited Los Angeles, we held on to the stereotype that L.A. is in its own sunny, flaky, movie bubble with little activist potential. After Emma and I spoke with a few of our peers, our assumptions went out the window. Our first couple days in L.A., we meet up with three young women involved in Hollywood: a filmmaker, an actress, and a screenwriter. All are very aware of how their gender affects their career and desires in the movie city.

Our hostess is Julia B., twenty-four, a documentary filmmaker who lives in Venice and is the daughter of film producer Laura Ziskin. She sees the job of director as a "position of control that women are almost afraid to want." In the film industry, she says, men challenge and question women's authority at every turn. One director she knows told her, "Ridley Scott can show up in his sweatpants. I have to go to work all dressed up." Julia is a feminist and says the extra pressure that women experience in the film industry needs to be addressed, especially since "woman directors often say that they direct the films they want to see" and women are a coveted demographic of moviegoers. She wants to organize a round table with mothers and daughters about feminism, because, Julia says, we should "try to revive this conversation."

Anna, twenty-two, is a young actress originally from the suburbs of Chicago who tells us that, as a woman, "the less talent you have, the more pressure you have to look good." She feels the demand to get ahead in the game while she's still young, while she's still perfect and pretty by Hollywood standards. She notices a difference in attitude between male and female actors, telling us that "confidence is the number one obstacle" for young women in the industry. And she does in fact see feminism and self-confidence as directly connected. Anna is a feminist because, she says, "Any woman, if she believes in herself, is a feminist." She goes on to state what we already know: that there are many more interesting roles for men, and that most scripts in Hollywood are geared toward male roles. "I just wish I was a screenwriter," she sighs.

Julia G., twenty-four, is in fact a screenwriter and definitely calls herself a feminist. She and a friend are in the middle of writing a screenplay—"sort of the female version of *Superbad*." She tells us that even great pieces of pop culture, from a female perspective, haven't quite gotten it right. "*Mean Girls*, for example, brought up a lot of important issues, but it basically said, 'Whether you're Janis or Regina, you're a bitch.' My friends are just as entertaining and engaging as guys we see on film. We curse a lot, we tell dirty jokes, too. My friend and I are writing a screenplay about women who are neither threatening nor boring."

JULIA B. (TOP); JULIE G. (MIDDLE); ANNA (BOTTOM)

HOLLYWOOD BOULEVARD

Marianna, Emma, and I end up walking miles and miles down the Hollywood strip. Lingerie shops are lit with the glow of slutty Halloween costumes, garter belts, lace and leather and nurse's crosses. The Walk of Fame bears the names of Mary Astor and Jim Hill, and reminds us of Hollywood's transient history—"Who the hell are these people?" We pass through billboards and lights, through Motorola and Mountain Dew and McDonald's. We shake hands with a giant Elmo and two men gilded with silver and gold lacquer. It is a scene that could be mistaken for Times Square were it not for the stretching palms and the looming Scientology tower.

—Nona

Lili

Lili, twenty-one, invites us for dinner in her parents' gorgeous house on a hill in Bel Air. Lili's parents are Persian Jews who came over from Iran during the revolution. They raised her in a very conservative, traditional household where she wasn't allowed to go out in high school or live in the dorms when she went to UCLA.

"You don't date someone unless you intend to marry them," Lili tells us. "And my parents want me to get married as soon as possible." They always encouraged her to have a career, but, she says, "Marriage is always the priority. Sometimes I think they want me to have a good job so that I'm more marketable to men." She notes that the same restrictions weren't put on her brothers, which frustrated her to no end. Because of this double standard, Lili considers herself a feminist. She learned about feminism in school and by picking up magazines like *Bitch*—"I found [the magazine] to be funny and interesting, and I liked looking at culture through that lens."

But Lili still adheres to many of her cultural traditions, telling any man she becomes involved with that he needs to be in it for the long haul, straight up. "Waiting to have sex until you're married is how I was raised, so I've come to believe it." Lili plans on marrying early "to finally be free," as she puts it. "Sometimes I think my parents are so hard on me just to make me want to get married." Is she going to incorporate any of these traditions with her own family? "I want to have some of the same rules about going out for my own children. But the rules will be the same for both boys and girls," she assures us.

LILI

CLAREMONT

Leaving Lili's, we are ready to get out of L.A. and on the road to Claremont. Marianna puts on the cheesy car tunes, and we start down the steep hills of Bel Air. All at once Billie Joe Armstrong is singing "She," my boyfriend calls, and Nona starts screaming. Before I know it, the car is tipping left, I have dropped the call, and I am clutching onto my MacBook for dear life. "What the fuck!" My first instinct is to crawl out of the car as soon as possible, assuming it is going to blow up. Nona and Mari follow. Nona was driving, and she is hysterical. "I have no idea what just happened! Omigod! The car just stopped working. The brakes wouldn't work!" Fortunately, all is well and AAA arrives on the scene in record time.

—**Emma**

Emma and Sarah

An hour later we are en route to Claremont, squished into the front seat of the AAA tow truck headed fifty miles south. We are starving and dazed and excited to get to Emma's. An old friend of mine from NYC, she moved out to Cali for school and has since made a full conversion to the laid-back warmth and sunny spirit of the West Coast. She and Sarah, also from out east, live in a typical hippied-out college apartment, filled with M.I.A. posters, empty beer bottles, and Mexican throws. They immediately offer us a crunchy feast, with glasses of wine and joints to boot, and soon we are finally sated and relaxed.

After one too many drinks, all of us escape into Emma's room for some privacy from the other roommates. We take our best stab at grilling Emma and Sarah through wine-stained lips. Both identify as feminists, but Sarah doesn't believe in one national identity of "American woman." Emma thinks there might be an essential thing that bonds us together as women: "I feel it, but can't put my finger on it." There is a spark in her eyes as she whispers intently, "My closest bonds are with my girlfriends." Then she pauses, looking confused: "But what if I am just brainwashed into saying or thinking there is such a thing as womanhood?" All of a sudden laughter erupts. In my best conspiracy voiceover I say, "What if we are just really stoned?" We start to giggle. It's time for bed.

—**Emma**

EMMA (LEFT) AND SARAH

SAN DIEGO

In San Diego we stay with Mike, a family friend, and are greeted with an outdoor hot tub, wet suits, and kick-ass Mexican food. We indulge in some much-needed revelry as we sip beer and smoke joints in the Jacuzzi with mid-'90s rock in the background. The weather is crisp and warm. The California cool floats through the air. We forget about interviewing for a night and, for a little moment, we're actually on vacation.

Becky

Mike hooks us up with Becky, one of his students at San Diego State. She talks rapid-fire and is one of the few young women we've interviewed who asserts that feminism is a huge part of her life. Starting by quoting Gloria Steinem, she states, "If you're not a feminist, you're a masochist." She goes on: "Your eyes are not open. Women who subscribe to the ideals but have trouble with the label—that shows a lack of maturity. People shouldn't be afraid of what other people think."

Becky is twenty, originally from Chicago and La Verne, California. She's in the midst of applying to law school to get involved in reproduction law and maybe become a lobbyist. She sees the problem of feminism's bad rep as directly correlated to education: "People should be educated on a high school level about what it means to be a feminist. What you don't know about doesn't exist, unless you think and talk about it—exactly what we're doing now."

Emma asks the question we're both thinking: "What about before high school? Some of the worst manifestations of toxic girl culture happen at a young age." During many a late-night conversation on this road trip, Emma and I have pinpointed middle school, hands down, as the time

BECKY

of our ultimate lows in confidence and self-esteem. All those teen magazines, body changes, spin-the-bottle, cliques, and shit-talking—god, it was terrible. Becky at first hesitates to admit that girl culture is a widespread issue, but she eventually comes around to admitting that "it's true—we are bred through the media, and society expects us to be all one way." Becky hopes that women will keep an eye out for themselves and their daughters, constantly questioning what we absorb, because "everyone should be their own cultural critic."

> "People should be educated on a high school level about what it means to be a feminist. What you don't know about doesn't exist, unless you think and talk about it." —Becky

Marilisa, Shannon, and Kristen

When we meet up with three other San Diego State ladies, all feminists, we discuss the possibility of a movement that includes men—after all, it does have a considerable effect on their lives, too.

Kristen, twenty-five, is originally from Modesto and San Jose, California, and is working on a PhD in public health. She thinks that feminism has been too limited and should definitely include men. "If feminism is ever going to work," she says, "everyone has to be involved."

Marilisa, twenty-seven and from Philly, is getting her master's and agrees. But, she adds, "Women should be the center of attention"—where feminism is concerned. Emma asks about the expansion of gender labels: "Isn't it a slippery slope when choosing who gets to be at the forefront of a movement?" Marilisa thinks for a

> **"If feminism is ever going to work, everyone has to be involved."** —Kristen

second, then says, "Then I guess we need to redefine what it means to be a woman and a man."

Kristen tells us, "There's always that fear that men will end up dominating the conversation." But Shannon, twenty-five, from Cali and Wisconsin, and also in the sociology masters program at San Diego State, points out, "It's not like the guys that would be involved in feminism would be misogynists."

Emma and I have been throwing these thoughts around for the past few weeks. "Should we be interviewing men?" we muse every time a feminist man posts a comment on our blog or we have a two-minute cell chat with one of our guy friends. On our way from California to the Southwest, we brainstorm a list of men we want to interview—mostly guys who are our dear friends but whom we would never date because they're assholes to girls. Or men who seem to defy gender labels and act as feminine or as masculine as they want. Or hipster dudes who, despite their gender-bending aesthetic, are more macho than you would think. Or . . . the thoughts race on. "There should be a femasculine movement," Emma quips in the car, only half-joking.

KRISTEN, MARILISA, AND SHANNON

CHAPTER 5 --- **Day Trippers**

LAS VEGAS

Creeping up to Las Vegas in the middle of the night, after hours on a clogged highway, we pass a few sad-looking strip joints before we arrive at our hotel. We have planned accordingly for Halloween night in Vegas, resolving to dress up as "scary feminists" and see what happens. We combed the thrift stores of San Diego to put together our ensembles: I was Bella AbZOMBIE, Emma was Emma GHOULman, and Marianna was Gloria DIEnem. Prepared to answer a lot of drunken questions about our costumes, we venture out on the glitzy Vegas Strip.

THE STRIP

We turn up the music real high in our hotel room and start a fashion show—get right for the night, primp, tuck. I put on my awesome frumpy '80s Bella Abzug dress. We gulp down alcohol and prepare for our first real party night in weeks, a total girls' night. It feels good not to have to look hot for Halloween. We garner some inane sexist comments, even worse than we expected. "What are you guys, spinsters?" "Hey, wanna cook my dinner?"

We're having fun until I start to get irrationally upset when Emma wriggles into her miniskirt in the middle of the street. Great, now I have the frumpiest costume of us three, I think. Emma sucks down more free drinks and bats her eyelashes at a guy who I have been talking to all night. I don't even like him, but that's not the point. I feel like our feminist Vegas night has just turned into the same shit it does in a New York bar—meat-market-style competition and drunkenness. It gets worse when the guys invite us to some hole-in-the-wall bar and we accept. Emma smooches one of them and Mari and I pull her away. My frustration precipitates, and I need to have a thirty-second cry in the bathroom. Why does it always boil down to this?

—Nona

GRAND CANYON

The Grand Canyon is a bitch to get to. The path leading to the south side of the Canyon is inundated with gravelly ridges, each bump threatening to slice our little Chevy's tires to bits. When we finally get there the normal tours are closed, but we finagle our way into the last private tour van. We are escorted into the gorge just in time for sunset, which makes for great photos (although every one seems absurd, like an imitation of a Kodak billboard). I can't stop thinking about Thelma & Louise and feeling kind of smug that we've made it this far and we're still doing okay. It is pitch-black when we leave and face the ripply road again. I can't wait to rest our heads on a Best Western pillow.

—*Nona*

 have been stuck in that car squashed between jabbering and jolts all day. I need to run into the setting sun as soon as the minivan reaches the Grand Canyon peak. Reaching for my camera, I realize that photographing this grandeur is pointless. I want to enjoy the moment for once. In twenty-four hours we have gone from one of the most clichéd American tourism destinations to one of the finest. But the Grand Canyon seems so perfect it could be faker than Vegas—its brick red stone illuminated by the sun like the red glow of the flashing signs, on and off, as the sun passes. A Native American guide describes how he comes here every morning and basks in the stillness. It does seem hollow, a pause in time. After three weeks of bouncing around, endlessly, restlessly busy and wandering, it inspires a cease in all activity. The layers of rock encapsulate infinity, arresting and calming.

—*Emma*

TUCSÓN

After dropping Mari off at the airport, now sick of staring at miles of desolate stretch, we reach the oasis of Tucson. We're staying with Emma's friend Luke, who'd recently moved to Tucson from Chicago for no particular reason. Two back-to-back interviews with older feminists await us on our first day. Emma and I have heard the cracks about the Southwestern, artsy, menopausal white women, but we have a feeling that our interview with Joanna, an erotic performance artist, will make us see things a little differently.

LUKE IN THE CACTII

Joanna

We meet with Joanna Frueh in her Tucson home, a fantastical and artfully retro adobe house. Joanna is an art historian and a performance artist who redefines the erotic. She is in her late fifties but has the energy, confidence, and sensuality of a newly desirous twenty-year-old. She puts us at ease by telling us how happy and optimistic she feels about our generation, which in some ways she relates to more than her own. "When I see women who look like you, I identify with you," she says. "I identify with the girliness, sexuality, the shapes and shapeliness, naturalness, your individuality and femininity."

Joanna tells us that younger women and Third Wave feminists are much more comfortable with her work, which includes talking graphically and romantically about orgasm and the erotic. "I was performing my one-woman show, *The Aesthetics of Orgasm,* in Belfast, and the audience was full of disapproving women my age. It is really something to be up there performing and feel such hostility from women." She feels that many Second Wave feminists don't "get" her eroticism and seem to be more focused on "the narrative of loss . . . suffering and shaming of the body."

Joanna has been in the Southwest for a while and was in Chicago in the late '70s, so she wasn't running into the kinds of Second Wave discussions that were going on in the heyday. But she has long identified as a feminist, remembering reading the feminist books in college and thinking, *I'm home.*

I am deeply inspired by Joanna and her breezy admission that sex is central all through a woman's life, not just during her youth. "Many older women just stop talking about sex. So many women resign to being unsexual as they get older," which, to Joanna, seems like giving in to cultural constrictions and dogmas about age. She contests the idea of needing to be genetically blessed to pull this off, telling us about a woman she knows who, though not conventionally attractive, drives men insane. But I'm skeptical. What *will* happen to my sex life when I get older? I pray that I can maintain a graceful sexuality that rivals Joanna's, one that helps reverse the cultural norm of the sexless grandma.

Secretly I start picturing, as I often do, how my life would be different if I didn't have certain beauty prerequisites—starting with my twenty-three-year-old skin. Would Joanna still see the "sexiness" and the "femininity" that she noticed as soon as we stepped out of our car? Part of me

JOANNA

says yes, yet I worry about the ways our image-conscious society refuses to see the inner sexuality radiating out of weathered sixty-year-old exteriors. I wonder if my generation can carve out a new way of seeing things based on how we want to see ourselves as we age. But isn't that what Joanna's generation once wanted for themselves, too?

Bailey

Bailey Doogan, a painter and feminist, was the first woman to teach in the art department at the University of Arizona. Bailey came to feminism because of the difficulty she experienced being a woman in the art world. Her work has never received the recognition it deserves, and she has been attacked for portraying the reality of aging women's bodies, which is "scary" to some critics. But for her, the work has always been about "beauty" and getting past "shame about the body." One person went so far as to call her "an angry aging bitch," a phrase she later reclaimed and incorporated into self-portraits.

A recent set of life-size self-portraits hangs in her studio. It is called "Self-Examination." Bailey has battled with various illnesses over the last year, challenging her sense of identity and stability. As we leave Bailey's, both Nona and I wonder what issues become important to feminists as they grow older and have to deal with a corrupt healthcare system and a society that idolizes youth. We are glad that artists like Bailey keep women visible—at all ages.

—**Emma**

BAILEY

Madeline and Liz

Madeline and Liz are roommates from Omaha, Nebraska, and Dayton, Ohio, respectively. Both are feminists and activists. They both work for Food Not Bombs. Liz also assists an environmental lawyer and has volunteered helping domestic abuse and rape victims; Madeline also works at an LGBT youth center and is an organizer of upcoming Tucson Trans Awareness Week.

Liz is from a progressive family and was raised Unitarian. "I saw gay couples at church, so I was aware from a young age of alternative lifestyles." She first experienced sexism in the activist groups and hardcore punk circles of Ohio. "I knew there was something wrong with all these boys ruling the mosh pit and the political arguments. I knew this something needed a name—and that was feminism." She continues, "It must be invisible to people, but women still have a lot to struggle with. We think we have choice, but there is a lot people don't want to admit."

> ## "We think we have choice, but there is a lot people don't want to admit." —Liz

Madeline learned about feminism and became connected to the vocabulary in high school, around the time she came out as a lesbian. Reading a lot of the history and theory gave her confidence in her opinions, which especially helped when she attended conservative University of Arkansas.

Madeline thinks people are afraid of organizing around a definable cause, but Liz notes, "The way you live your life is just as important as being an activist." She does think there are "hints" on the horizon of a new movement, she gives a big smile. "It'd be fucking rad if there was one."

—*Emma*

LIZ (LEFT); MADELINE (RIGHT)

PHOENIX

While Emma takes care of some photographic business in Tucson, I wake up early to drive to our next interviewee. An hour away from the offbeat adobe houses of Tucson is an entirely different beast: the scorching suburban sprawl of Phoenix. Quirky little coffee shops quickly transform to Starbucks and McDonald's. As I pass through Scottsdale, a town that a friend of mine once called the "Beverly Hills of the Southwest," the streets are dotted with designer boutiques and spas. I meet Siman at a taqueria that's out of the ritzy part but still nestled between a parking lot and a RadioShack.

Siman

Siman tells me straight up over tacos that she does not relate to feminism. Siman was born in Somalia, went to Howard University, and works for the public health department. Siman is a single mom raising a small daughter in Phoenix, where she grew up. She doesn't identify as a feminist because "the world is most divided along class and race lines. The battles most important to me are globalization and capitalism." As a Muslim woman, Siman thinks that gender equality is not a priority "when you feel that your entire culture is under attack." But Siman does see empowering women as key to developing world societies.

> **"Islam bumped up against my core beliefs. When you get down to the bare bones of Islam, women are just *not* equal."** —Siman

"When you unleash the power of 50 percent of the population, things have to get better and change," she tells me.

Siman feels a strong connection to her cultural heritage. At one point she became very religious, after her divorce when she was working at a center helping Somalian refugees. "I came into fundamentalist Islam in order to get back to basics," she says. She explained to her shocked parents, who are devoted Marxists, "You're for the proletariat? Well, the proletariat believes in God." But eventually, she confesses, "Islam bumped up against my core beliefs. When you get down to the bare bones of Islam, women are just *not* equal. I actually started thinking, *Am I less? This can't be.* But it's hard to give up my religion and culture. It's a pull of allegiances."

When I ask her about being a single mother, Siman answers, "Now this is where we need feminism to come in. We just have too much damn work." Siman says that truthfully, it wasn't all that different when she was married. "Men help out, but in little niches. We are still the ones managing the households." Siman plans to reconcile with her husband, who lives in the Bahamas. Describing her husband as traditional in many ways, she says, "I see value in different gender roles if they are based on skill. Woman and men are better at different things—that's what makes humanity interesting."

SIMAN WITH HER DAUGHTER SAFIYA

SANTA FE AND ABIQUIU

We set out driving to Abiquiu, the town where Emma's family friend Mei-mei has a retreat away from the raucous streets of New York. In a departure from our usually precise mapping from our BlackBerry, we have some hastily written instructions scrawled from a phone conversation with Mei-mei. We are worried we won't get there before it gets pitch-black—something our hostess has warned us about. When we finally make it up the steep, rocky path to our destination, we see the fruits of our labor. Glowing on the high desert plain is Mei-mei's famously sparse abode built with completely natural materials and our digs for the next few days—a matching minimal-ist guesthouse.

Mei-mei

We interview Mei-mei Berssenbrugge over tea the next morning on her sunny balcony overlooking a timeless Southwest landscape. Mei-mei is sixty and has a regal and wise air about her. She is draped in an angular cream tunic, and her calm pointedness resembles the Agnes Martin paintings that hang in her bedroom. She was born in Beijing and comes from a long line of strong women, her grandmother being one of the first women to have a university education in China. "These dandelions are like a yellow blanket," Mei-mei uttered at age five, beginning her long career as a poet.

She was the first Chinese American woman on record to publish a volume of poetry, and she very much considers herself a feminist. Mei-mei remained completely focused on her career until, at age forty-two, she had her daughter, who is "the most significant person" in her life now. She sees an overcompetitive, overstressed pressure on our generation and believes we don't have enough time to figure out who we are, which will inevitably affect modern feminism. She doesn't feel much allegiance to "European principles of heroic individuality," intuiting that a new feminism should "change the worldview to be more about unity and connectedness. Gender now has only elements of convention rather than any absolute."

—**Emma**

MEI-MEI

LoSS

Mei-mei's words echo in our minds throughout the day as we explore the ancient Bandelier cave dwellings, climbing inside the porous rouge rocks and fantasizing about how the landscape of American feminism has changed over the years. Later that night in town we interview two male painters—Cisco, an old friend and self-proclaimed feminist, and Ryan, a domineering caricature of a manipulative chauvinist who tells us we are "too pretty to be feminists." He tells us we are creating more "boxes" with our trip, instead of focusing on the "spiritual" oneness of humanity, which, in his worldview, includes a fundamental difference between men and women. "I man, you woman"

style. Although I get angry enough to tell him, "You are the reason I cannot sleep at night," we all become friends by the end, even having an impromptu car stereo dance party in the streets of Santa Fe. Mei-mei did say humans alternate between "duality and unity." Is this an example?

We leave the boys and head to a nearby Borders parking lot to do our usual routine: pick up a free wi-fi signal and sit in our office (the car) entangled in cords and lit by the glow of our Macs. It's then when I realize my camera has disappeared. After the hysteria peaks, I try to put it into perspective given what we've learned since being with Mei-mei. Our brand of feminism and self-discovery has been so tainted by technology and the fear of loss it creates. The immediacy that the Internet and all things digital provide has cut off an arm of real experience, trumping virtual validation over lived reflection. But these are the tools we have, and my camera is most certainly our eyes.

—*Emma*

ACID

Emma's blue backpack is a grab bag containing countless skin products, DVDs, and intoxicants—among them a couple acid tabs. We return to Abiquiu and drop acid at midnight, popping in *The Graduate* to bide the time. Mei-mei's spaceshiplike guesthouse feels like going back to basics after weeks of image overload. The tassels on the rug start to tremble just as the story approaches its creepy finale, where Elaine and Ben flee from the wedding, their eyes asking each other, "So we fucked the system—what do we do now?" We are consumed by a feeling of contentment, marveling at what we've done so far.

An hour into the trip, we are the most joyful and solid we've felt in weeks. We're forced to unclutter our brains. "New York really drives people to this minimalism," Emma jokes. We take ludicrous photos on our MacBook and laugh until our stomachs hurt, like little girls on a play date. So different from Kerouac's beer-drenched joyrides or Hunter S. Thompson's druggy, paranoid wonderland. The stereotype of the freewheeling road trip, the revelry of *Fear and Loathing in Las Vegas*. What a joke—not us at all. Instead of getting wasted every night, we have been writing blog entries, making last-minute changes to our itinerary, winding down after sixteen-hour days. Now, after all that, we are finally us.

—*Nona*

CHAPTER 6 - - **That Endless Skyway** →

DENVER

Browsing a used bookstore in Seattle, we impulsively bought the recorded version of Jack Kerouac's *On the Road*, but since then we hadn't had the time to burn it onto our iPods. Now's our chance as we drive the six hours to Denver from Abiquiu. We've each read the book and remembered liking it, but now with feminism on the brain, we're smarting at the anachronistic way Kerouac talked about women. Why must every female character be so slutty, stupid, and superfluous? We realize Kerouac was "of his time," but America's documented history of the road trip starts to seem more masculine than ever.

Still, we feel a connection with him for dropping everything and hitting the open road, especially when the narrator describes the "great sea-plain of Denver" just as we begin cruising down the city's Colfax Avenue, surrounded by both glitzy condos and looming mountains. The freewheeling road trip may be more Beat than Gen Y, but one thing hasn't changed: the amazement of laying eyes on a new city for the first time.

Szoke

Szoke is a friend from high school who moved to Denver from New York less than a year ago. It was technically because her boyfriend was moving here, but she tells us that it was more that she needed a change and this was her chance. Now, she tells us, "I feel like I'm on vacation—both because I'm so happy and because I'm taking a break from the career thing." Szoke, a waitress, has always wanted to be an actress but has never made that drastic move to really pursue it. "Sometimes I think acting is subconsciously not what I want to do. It's important to me to think of what else I'd be happy doing," she says. Psychiatry and teaching come to mind because Szoke wants to "affect people's lives in a positive way." Szoke, like many other women, wavers on the feminist question because she believes in the ideals but isn't "doing anything about it."

We get to shooting the shit about her job, and she tells us she "had the worst night of waitressing ever" last night. An older man—a "slimeball with a wedding ring"—flirted with her all night, but when it came to ordering and his food, he was completely condescending. "He was making sure I knew what I was doing because I must be stupid if I'm a waitress." Knowing that type of customer all too well (I've been a waitress on and off for years), I ask what she thinks of women's position in the service industry. Szoke, who makes more money than her boyfriend, answers, "Sometimes I can't believe I have a job that allows people to treat me like that, but I like interacting with people. Waitressing is good money and usually easy. Male waiters are more respected, though. There are always going to be those people who get off on the idea that a woman is serving them."

> "Male waiters are more respected. There are always going to be those people who get off on the idea that a woman is serving them." —Szoke

SZOKE

KANSAS CITY

After getting two speeding tickets in a row, Emma just wants to get to Kansas City by bedtime. We are staying with her old friend, Craig, who lived in New York back when she was in her teens. A week or two beforehand, we had grilled him for ideas of interviewees in his native city. "Believe me," he assured us, "I have some amazing friends you can talk to, girls who have been through a lot." It's only the next day, upon meeting Monica, when we see what he meant.

Monica

Monica, twenty-five, was raised in Texas and Kansas, born to "free spirit" Mexican Indian father and an immigrant German mother. "I was always interested in art and photography," she tells us, "but I didn't have an outlet for it, so I joined the military right out of high school and studied air traffic. My mom begged me not to go, but I make really rash decisions. It was free college, and it was a quick and easy way to leave home."

Monica knows exactly why she isn't a feminist: "I'm raunchy. I'm insulting. I'm sexually harassing. I exploit women. I want to grow up and make my house all pretty and plant flowers, just sit and drink and not have to bust my ass." But most of all, she tells us, "I don't view issues as a woman. I don't separate things in terms of gender. Sometimes I feel androgynous. I really feel that I can live my life equally."

I am surprised at first that Monica's experience in the military, the ultimate emblem of brute, masculine power, did not make her think twice about her position as a woman. But as she gives us the excruciating blow-by-blow of boot camp, technical school, and being in a correctional facility after getting busted with alcohol, I begin to understand. Whether you're a man or a woman in the military, you're subjugated no matter what. Every soul answers to the same authority, and egos are stepped on regardless of sex organs. Clearly she's

a woman who refuses to make it easy on herself—joining the military even while she says, "I don't like being told what to do." Monica seems more interested in overcoming obstacles rather than pandering to any sense of identity.

At one point, Monica was sent to prison for four months for smoking pot. There was no space in the military facility, so she was sent to a county jail in North Dakota where 80 percent of those incarcerated were Native American—many of them women. She watched people leave and come back, losing children to the authorities every day. "Some of them would get irritated with me, like *Oh, poor air force girl got in trouble,* but we also kinda got along. We made trades, like lotion for colored pencils." Emma asks if she felt connected to the women she was in prison with, and Monica shakes her head. "I made the best of it, but no, I didn't feel connected to them."

Monica does not fit any GI Jane stereotype, exuding a caustic, bohemian vibe. She came back to Kansas after prison to get her degree as an art teacher, but eventually the school refused to fund her education because of the felony on her record. The only tinge of regret we pick up on is when Monica reveals this recent setback. "I took a lot of things from being in the military," she says, but the fact that she can't finish her teaching degree makes her question those years. It makes her sad because, as she puts it, "I really think I have a lot to give."

MONICA

JOEY (TOP); ANGELA (BOTTOM)

Angela and Joey

Angela and her friend Joey meet us at Monica's house for a cup of coffee. Angela, twenty-six, is originally from Kansas City, and although she plans to open a boutique and gallery with Craig, her boyfriend, she has a degree in biology and is now working at a lab. Joey, twenty-three, grew up in Denver, wants to be a costume designer, and now sews and crafts freelance wherever she can. They both tentatively consider themselves feminists, but also shy away from the term because of the negative stereotypes. We get to talking about how each of their professions are generally associated with one gender over another.

Joey: "I'm surrounded by gay guys and women. Little boys don't sit around thinking about being a costume designer—or maybe they're not allowed to. I'm sure a lot of men liked it in college but would never major in it because they wouldn't want a negative label. I think women have passed men in the ability to blend gender roles."

Angela: "Yeah, because men feel like they would lose more, while we only have things to gain. Science teachers would say to the women students, 'Prove them

> *"I think women have passed men in the ability to blend gender roles."* —Joey

wrong that men are better at science.' But in the workplace the doctors are overwhelmingly male, and the nurses are mostly women. I think it's because nurses get shit on all the time, and also because they're seen as more maternal. Its funny, though—women nurses are always encouraging other women to go into the profession."

Maria

Flustered and late, we are greeted with breakfast at Maria Elena Buszek's house on a street lined with autumn leaves. Maria, a Third Waver, has been a feminist since age nine, when a new papal law banned her from being an altar girl in late-'70s Detroit. "Does the pope think we're not as good as boys?" she asked the adults around her, and she realized that "this gender thing was a big deal." Raised in a Catholic family, she says her dad's "denigrating comments about feminism indicated that it was a powerful, righteous thing."

She is a professor of art history at the Kansas City Art Institute and is the author of *Pin-Up Grrrls,* which explores the history of the pin-up and its long-standing connection to feminism. She is now working on a book, inspired by some of her crafty students, that is "bridging the art/craft divide" and acknowledging the cohort of artists who are experimenting with craft media. She says that "domestic media" (the subject of her first book) is a concept that "some faculty just doesn't get." It pisses her off when academia hastily judges whether a topic or a piece of art is feminist or not. Emma fervently agrees. In her senior thesis, Emma examined the 1999 exhibit Another Girl, Another

> **"We have to find out what leads women to believe in the power of** showing their boobs **at Mardi Gras if they can't even ask for a raise at work."** —Maria

Planet, a group show by young women photographers whose glossy, fashiony images were harshly criticized for perceived misogyny and superficiality. Maria rolls her eyes. "The minute artists use titillation to attract journalists, they get attacked for it. The press says, 'These are the only images I will pay attention to, but how dare you create these images?'"

I bring up the *Girls Gone Wild* phenomenon. Does she think sexual empowerment has gone too far? "Some women do see this as liberating, but it seems to be an uninformed feeling of power," Maria says. "What we have to find out is what leads these women to believe in the power of showing their boobs at Mardi Gras if they can't even ask for a raise at work." But she thinks it's disrespectful to young women for older feminists to "take the scolding route, to assume that these women don't know what they're doing." She has a lot of faith in our generation, but "simply reclaiming one's sexuality is never enough; it's the narcissistic, Courtney Love 'feminism for one.' Young women should be aware that their sexuality is a public matter."

MARIA

craig in
kansas city   11-7-07   3:31 am

emma in
kansas city   11-7-07   3:30am

NIGHT AT CRAIG'S HOUSE

From the start, we've been eager to get our guy friends involved in our project, but we didn't know how. We've only discussed *Girldrive* with men a handful of times on our trip, and most of them (with the exception of drama queen Ryan in the Southwest) shrugged and held their tongues. They seemed to hint that they felt overwhelmed by the whole thing, that their opinion didn't matter, or that we didn't want it.

Craig gives his position freely the second night we all chill, drinking and talking until four in the morning.

"I feel insecure about claiming feminism," he tells us, perhaps echoing the thoughts of the hesitant boys we had encountered along the way. "Even if I feel sympathetic to it, it is not my movement to own. I more see myself as a male operating between two extremes, two gender lines. I don't think the movement ended. It never went away."

We're curious for him to go on, to offer a male perspective on feminism in our culture. "I see feminism as an ongoing industry, created and needing to be maintained," he explains. "There is nothing wrong per se with the feminism industry (magazines, books, classes, products), but it can objectify the issue, turn it back on itself. It seems that the feminist industry can create a dangerous political correctness."

We nod at that last characterization—Emma and I had spent late nights bemoaning the straight-faced PCness that is equated with Second Wave feminism, although we had a hunch that Craig was less familiar with younger feminists and their playfulness.

One thing was clear: Now, more than ever, we need sympathetic men to be opinionated, to call us out on the effectiveness of feminism and its PR department. Even though Emma and I won't let go of the word itself, laden with history and still imbued with power, we recognize the need to redefine these issues so that men like Craig, men who are potential allies, will feel compelled to participate.

ST.LÓUIS

Óur stopover in St. Louis is purely for a break and marks the halfway point of the road trip. Emma has made arrangements to visit her boyfriend, so I call a friend from college to see if I can stay in her parents' house when they are on vacation. In a big house with no one to talk to, I have plenty of time to think—especially since this day of rest marks the one-year anniversary of my mother's death.

dRIvIng

My mother, journalist, feminist, and cultural critic Ellen Willis, died exactly one year before our night in St. Louis, halfway through *Girldrive*'s journey. I honor her by reliving the few weeks after her death—during which I obsessively sifted through writing by her and about her. After her funeral, it was sensory overload for weeks on end, not only because responses to death are emotional hurricanes, but because every lazy, indeterminate goal I had to be both a writer and a feminist suddenly came alive. I began filling in the blanks in my knowledge about the Women's Movement. I learned how it had literally started from a few women realizing they had common ground and deciding to talk about it. It was a crash course in American feminism, a history lesson in the form of anecdotes, tearful elegies, and primary documents.

At the same time, people who had been affected by my mother's work all felt drawn to me, to fill the space Mom had left behind. They handed me letters, old papers, photos, pamphlets from feminist conferences, old issues of The Village Voice containing scathing critiques in my mother's weekly column. Among the people who felt a need to reach out to me, to take me out to dinners and lunches and explain who my mother was, were her old friends from the Women's Movement, many of them notable feminists and many of them childless.

There's a whole generation of feminists, of fifty- and sixtysomething women, who never had children. They will say it's for various reasons—their intellectual life took precedence, they just didn't feel it was the right time, or it wasn't important to them. But there's also an unspoken sense of "I was a feminist, not a mother," a sentiment I am happy to say, thanks to the Third Wave Superwoman, has almost disappeared. Judging by my mother's friends, though, there remains an urge to reach out to the next generation—even if they don't always realize it.

My mother almost didn't have me. She was thirty-nine and settled down with my dad when she asked tentatively, "You wouldn't want to have a child, would you?" Lucky for me, he was down. But for a long time she was resigned to the fact that she wasn't going to have kids. Kids seemed in conflict with her escape from domestic traps. But once I was born, her level of devotion was amazing. I know she often wondered why she ever thought feminism and motherhood were in conflict.

A day after Mom died, NPR replayed an interview she did in 1989—I was five at the time—on the how being a mother had affected her brand of feminism. For some reason, I had never gotten around to listening to it. I stumbled upon it on the one-year anniversary of her death, and my heart stopped when I heard this part:

"I think Stanley [my father] and I do our best in good faith to try to share everything. But then there always are things, like I really have a driving phobia . . . and I definitely know that it's connected with all sorts of things about femaleness. So Stanley does virtually all of the driving when we're in the city together. Nona has been seeing this . . . At one point, she even said to me, 'You have to have a penis to drive, right, Mama?' This is really on my agenda as a big thing that I have to deal with . . . I try to make her understand that this is just my weirdness. Now she sort of sits in the driver's seat and she pretends that she's driving and she really wants to learn to drive. The most important thing is that she should get the idea that it's great for her to try to do."

And I did get that idea. I never questioned that I could get my license and have a car. For the last year, I've been dependent on my driver's license to finish the most important thing I've ever done in my life. History is most easily passed on through family. Feminist history means a lot to Emma and me largely—albeit not completely—because of our mothers, who struggled to balance their professional lives with raising us. I'm hoping that somehow Mom can see that she did it right.

Tulsa

MELODY AND MANA

Austin

BIG STAR BURLESQUE

ELSA, LAURIE, AND ERIKA

CARMEN

CHAPTER 7 **Grass Routes**

TULSA

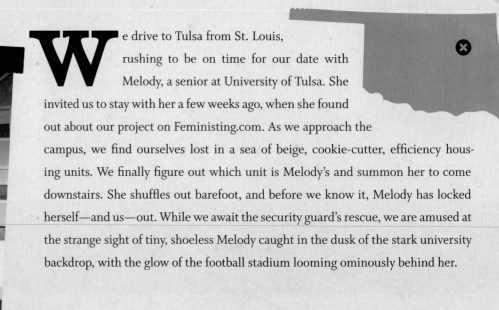

We drive to Tulsa from St. Louis, rushing to be on time for our date with Melody, a senior at University of Tulsa. She invited us to stay with her a few weeks ago, when she found out about our project on Feministing.com. As we approach the campus, we find ourselves lost in a sea of beige, cookie-cutter, efficiency housing units. We finally figure out which unit is Melody's and summon her to come downstairs. She shuffles out barefoot, and before we know it, Melody has locked herself—and us—out. While we await the security guard's rescue, we are amused at the strange sight of tiny, shoeless Melody caught in the dusk of the stark university backdrop, with the glow of the football stadium looming ominously behind her.

Melody and Mana

Melody, twenty-one, has invited her friend Mana, a graduate of TU, to the interview. She tells us, "I fell in love with Tulsa when I realized I could do a lot of good here." Mana, twenty-four, was born in Oklahoma after her parents paid a smuggler to bring them over from Iran. Both women identify as feminists. Mana came to feminism "through a natural progression of being socially conscious." She jokes that her "heart bleeds for everybody," and she shares how people don't get how she, a straight woman, works at an LGBT nonprofit. "Justice issues are all kinda the same—everyone deserves access to resources."

Melody possesses an intensity that is countered only by her delicate brown ringlets, porcelain skin, and glassy green eyes. She was raised in Colorado Springs in a traditionally Christian household and has only just recently realized her own "click" feminist moment. In her most serious yet understated tone she shares, "I know this sounds religious, but feminism saved my life." We crane forward for the story. "I was in this abusive

"I know this sounds religious, but feminism saved my life" —Melody

relationship, and everyone around me was telling me to get out. But I was in denial for so long, really isolated . . . then I started reading stuff about feminism and looking at blogs and Live-Journals. They were consciousness raising 'safe spaces' where people would talk about parallel situations to mine. They were just a place to vent." Mana murmurs from the couch, "God bless the Internet."

Melody says that if it were the 1970s and her only option was to go to a consciousness raising group, she would have never made it. The Internet made her realize that she wasn't alone, but "plugged in to something larger." As she was coming to terms with her own abusive relationship, she discovered that her mother was contemplating divorce. "She had a strict, controlling husband and was a stay-at-home mom for eleven years because it was the good, Christian thing to do, but she made it clear to me that she had regrets and didn't want the same thing to happen to me."

Both of these young women agree that the blogosphere is where feminism really thrives; it's a place where, as Mana puts it, "the words are more important than the faces."

We sit for an hour or so in a pot-induced haze. Emma is enraptured and silent while I press Melody for more details. As the night winds down and Emma and I drift off to sleep, I know we'll never think of our blog the same again.

MANA (TOP); MELODY (BOTTOM)

AUSTIN

At night we reach the outskirts of Austin, an area studded with strip malls bathed in the neon lights of sketchy-looking Chinese restaurants. We are en route to meet Big Star Burlesque, a plus-size dance troupe. The ladies are packed onto an L-shaped couch in the living room, with several husbands and boyfriends in tow. I immediately sense their community comfort; these girls regularly gather to sew costumes, brainstorm ideas, and strip together. From the photo studio in Raine's front room to the costumes and makeup strewn across the floors and countertops, it's clear that burlesque is more than a hobby for them.

—*Emma*

Big Star Burlesque

Florinda, twenty-nine, speaks up first. She is a "playwright, artist, activist, singer, educator"—a through-and-through Texas girl, raised outside of Houston. She works for the nonprofit Theatre Action Project. She is a feminist—although "not an equalist," she tells us: "I would fight in solidarity for women to do anything, but that doesn't mean I would want to go fight in the war."

Raine is twenty-two, was born in Austin, and has been doing burlesque for a year. She is a head seamstress for SewSister.com (a lingerie company) and dabbles in phone sex for extra money on the side. Her stage name is Sugar Cooky. She thinks of herself as a "modern, hip feminist," one who got married when she was twenty because she wanted to, not because she was "pregnant or pressured." She is the self-proclaimed "skinny bitch of the group." Big Star has allowed her to feel accepted—finally—since she didn't feel that her average frame fit in with skinny women or plus-size women. "I see Big Star as a size acceptance troupe," she tells us.

Cait has a tough-girl edge about her—her stage name is Kerosene—but her porcelain skin and soft baby fat give away her age. "I'm eighteen," she tells us. "I just moved here a month ago to meet my boyfriend," whom she met online. She is from Michigan, and since dropping out of high school, she's worked with Raine at SewSister.com. "I

dropped out of high school purely because I stopped learning in that education system," she explains. "On my own and in a smaller amount of time, I've learned far more than what they could have told me." She jokes, "I don't need a piece of paper telling me I'm more 'smartful' than before." She's a feminist—"not an extreme feminist, but what Raine said . . . a modern one."

Rebecca, twenty-two, is originally from California and has been in Austin for two years. She's a corporate recruiter by day— "every other day is a struggle to the top"— but doesn't want to stereotype herself as a feminist. She leaves it at that.

Originally from Queens, Stephanie, twenty-nine, is the founder and "mother hen" of Big Star. She came up with the idea a year ago. She was always interested in pin-ups but, as a larger woman, she had to find a venue for it. Now she runs a full variety show and is a telephone dominatrix—"the best-paid acting job I ever had"—where she can make upwards of $2.00 a minute.

Stephanie started the troupe because she wanted plus-size ladies to feel "freedom in their own skin." Her family never made her ashamed of her size, but she always felt like she had to remind herself,

STEPHANIE

CAIT (TOP); RAINE (BOTTOM)

'Be careful, keep covered.' Stephanie tells us that Big Star has more of a feminist slant than other troupes because it presents big women as "normal, beautiful, sensual, bold, campy, smart, sexy, and entertaining," without having to be merely "sassy ladies or comedic fodder. We bring a lot of wit and satire to the whole thing."

Most of the women had a "lightbulb" moment when they realized they wanted to do burlesque. Rebecca saw it as a chance to "get her femininity back," having been raised in an environment where women were the breadwinners. Florinda saw it as a way to make other bigger women feel sexy. Florinda gained weight later in life and realized how embarrassed other big women felt. She wanted a venue where she could tell them, "You ain't seen a big girl like this before." Cait adds, "Burlesque was a huge feminist step. It seemed to be a stab at the status quo."

I ask them why burlesque is often considered more "feminist" than, say, stripping. The consensus is that it's primarily a female-run industry and concept; also there's a conscious decision to participate that sets it apart from stripping—since so many strippers are working to make a living at it. Here the ladies make a distinction between class and education. With the exception of Stephanie, none of the women in the troupe have a college degree, but all make enough money to sacrifice a Sunday to practice burlesque. "We're all here by choice and don't have to be working that third job," Stephanie says. Florinda agrees. "We get to practice art. And I've always recognized art as a privilege." All the women agree that living in Austin gives them easy access to an intellectual, liberal environment. Cait tells us the reaction she gets when she explains to her friends what she's doing: "Wait, so you're a stripper who works at a factory?" But for her, this is way more about finding "a way to feel empowered, independent, and sexy, regardless of size or interest."

As the interview draws to a close, I pull Stephanie aside and ask about the phone sex. "I see it as a voice-acting job," she tells me. "I don't see it as degrading or empowering. On one hand, you have a lot of control over the situation. Then again, they *do* care a lot about what you look like." She rolls her eyes. "There's a whole industry of putting a face to the voice, and I use other women's pictures for myself. The fact is, I know I can make more money as a twenty-two-year-old Asian girl than a size 24 almost thirty-year-old."

Elsa, Laurie, and Erika

As we settle into Austin, we realize that Texas activists are a different breed entirely. We have three appointments back to back with native Texans, all of whom feel an urgency to put into action the change they want to see. Elsa, the chief-of-staff for State Representative Trey Martinez Fischer, chose the world of politics to pursue what she believes in. She grew up in the border town Pharr, surrounded by strong Mexican women and an activist father. "Immigrant women are *tough*," she assures us. "The myth in Mexican culture about women being the weaker sex is a crock." She is a feminist, putting issues like sexual health and family planning in the forefront of her politics. She acknowledges that she took a very different path from the women she grew up with. "A lot of my friends from the valley have kids and are married. They finished a few years of high school and that's about it. I don't plan on getting married unless it just happens that way."

Elsa splits her time between Austin and San Antonio, which makes her contemplate the dynamic of activism in each place. "It can be soul-killing to organize outside of Austin," she says, "but it's tough to be in an urban area where the

same ideas are thrown around." Mostly she sees her job as "connecting the dots," and besides convincing the other side, "work[ing] with like-minded groups to build coalitions." Elsa is hopeful about the future of feminism. "If you're an organizer, you have to be optimistic about change . . . or else you might as well get off the wagon right now."

The next day, we rush to meet Laurie, the twenty-six-year-old political director of Texas's branch of NARAL. I was practically born with a pro-choice stance as a left-wing New Yorker, but I am dying to hear how this logic flies in Texas. Laurie was born and raised in both Austin and South Texas. She has spent years committed to pro-choice activism in Texas, which,

ELSA (TOP); LAURIE (BOTTOM)

> # "Of course I am a feminist, but I would never call myself a feminist at the Capitol. Why poke that hornet's nest?"
>
> —Laurie

ERIKA

unbeknownst to me until today, is a state where abortion and reproductive rights apparently get "tested out" before spreading to other states. "Texas is a touchstone for the South," Laurie says. "Often we're tasked to do something that literally no one else has done." *Is that true for feminism, too?* I wonder. Would a few young Molly Ivinses and Ann Richardses be able to spread feminism down here like wildfire?

Laurie reaches out to diverse groups by arguing in logical, relatable terms. "Of course I am a feminist—everyone is entitled to what everyone else has. . . . But I would never call myself a feminist at the Capitol," she says. "Why poke that hornet's nest? I tell people, 'Texas is the number one state for teen pregnancy—at least we can all agree on pregnancy prevention, right?'"

Meanwhile, she says, she frames the issue differently when talking with Mexican American women in border towns. Condemning teenage pregnancy is "not appropriate," Laurie says; in communities where young pregnancy is part of the culture, she frames the issue as the right to prenatal healthcare. She admits to us that it's a hard job pushing the organization's policy agenda in Texas. "I'm twenty-six years old and I'm debating senators twice my age. . . . But I have to remember that I know this issue more than they do." No matter whom she is talking to, her Texas roots come in handy. "I'm aware, and I think it comes across to people, that I'm sweeping my own doorstep."

Finally, we drive to meet Erika in East Austin at the offices of PODER—People Organized in Defense of Earth and her Resources. Erika, twenty-seven, grew up in the border town of Eagle Pass in a trailer park. Her father was a Tejano musician and her mother worked at Wal-Mart for many years before she got her teaching degree, a goal that Erika also pursued. But later, Erika became involved with PODER. The organization was started by a group of Chicanos to challenge environmental injustices in East Austin, an area to which people of color were once forcibly relocated. PODER was initially equally male and female, but women "really stuck around, and now have become the mothers of the organization."

Erika would have called herself a feminist a few years ago but now feels less comfortable

> ## "We need a transformation of the aggression that seems natural to men." —Carmen

with the title. "I call myself a woman or a woman of color . . . but also I don't have a problem with the term 'Chicana feminist.'" She connects some of her environmental work to being a woman because "we see our earth as female," but she acknowledges that feminism isn't a priority for most women. "If you asked the women of Juárez facing femicide if they were feminists, they would say, 'I don't care, I'm just trying to get my children back.'"

Carmen

Tonight we share pints with Carmen in a balmy beer garden in West Austin. Carmen, a friend from college, came to Austin after she graduated, seeking the progressive community and organizations here.

Carmen works with Erika at PODER. Her parents, who raised her in Austin, are both activists and musicians and taught her that her environment and food are political issues. She sees class and race issues trumping feminism: "Movements are always going to have identity lines, especially when peoples are not imprisoned the same way." She still feels the need for balance between masculinity and femininity. "We need a transformation of the aggression that seems natural to men, that causes abuse in relationships and the violence born of war."

—Emma

CARMEN

AcTIvISM BEYoND THE TwO CoASTS

Since Tulsa, we've been noticing that being a feminist seems to mean a lot more to women from worlds where feminism is a foreign concept. The small oases in the middle of generally conservative areas are the places that make the biggest impact on us. Take Austin, a well-known liberal refuge plopped in the middle of a vast conservative state, or tolerant, quirky New Orleans. Their adversaries aren't a plane ride away—they are right there, a few miles down the road. What we've noticed in making our way through these towns is how much the future of feminist activism largely rests in the hands of radical community organizers in red states.

The West Coast, parts of New England, and New York City have always been the bastions of progressive thought, conjuring up images of hippies wearing Birkenstocks, determined picket-liners, or throngs of artsy young hipsters.

It's an entirely different story with the women we've met in the South or the Midwest. Laurie, Elsa, Carmen, and Erika, all Texas ladies from birth, are highly aware that they're, as Laurie put it, "sweeping [their] own doorstep." Both Laurie and Elsa shuttle between Austin and the "real" Texas, where not everyone is as kind to the concept of feminism. About her political work, Laurie tells us, "When these senators want to make antiquated laws about women, I'm sorta like, 'I know these guys. I grew up with these guys. I know how they feel about girls.' I feel more equipped to deal with them." Many of these women, especially those raised in economically failing areas, feel the need to think locally.

Affinity to one's own community creates native feminist activists in cities where the ideas are needed most. Melodee, from the east side of Flint, and Carmen and Sarah, from Detroit, all said that they had no plans to leave their cities. These women are persevering in their hometowns even though these cities are on the verge of collapse. Sarah told us that there's a "very macho feeling" in industrial Detroit. "Women will be essential to changing this city," she promises.

Although there is overlap, there's a distinction between leftist and class-based activism. Melodee and Sarah, from Michigan, aren't battling as much political opposition—since they live in a swing state with a strong Democratic presence in its cities. Erika's local work in liberal Austin is also sheltered from the conservatism of the rest of Texas. But these women are living among a population battling poverty and industrial decay, which is an issue that unilaterally affects women more than men. Regardless of whether their local action is motivated by political ideals or a need for an economic resurgence, many women are identifying obstacles right in their home states—and for this reason many feel an urge to stay there.

For those women who weren't born in rural, conservative, or poor areas, there is always the dilemma: Do I stay where people's values most coincide with mine, or do I try to make a difference in places where there is a shortage of feminist ideas? Ingrid, raised by a lefty New York family, picked up and moved to Austin because she was sick of the East Coast bubble. She chose to go to the University of Texas because she "got fed up with pretending to be living in Greenwich Village in the '20s." She wanted to do investigative reporting on race relations in the deep South.

This is not to discredit both the symbolic and real power that sprawling, all-inclusive liberal cities bring to the feminist scene. Places like New York and San Francisco, the centers of bigger, well-known feminist organizations, will always be useful networks and essential allies for young women working in conservative and poor areas. However, as it stands now, many of the better-known organizations and groups are working on a theoretical basis without getting their hands dirty. Kate, an anarchist midwife from New Orleans, became disillusioned by this disconnect after her stint at a national women's nonprofit. "Nonprofits like Planned Parenthood delay and control resources," she said, which was eventually why she rejected institutional feminism and chose to express herself through midwifery.

Grassroots organizers must forge connections with institutions that have the reputation and money to render them more visible. The future of feminism depends on a combination of a well-developed infrastructure and the fresh verve of women who battle blatant misogyny every day. —*Nona*

CHAPTER 8 - - **American Gothic** - - ➡

NEW ÓRLEANS

Before we settle in New Orleans, we pick up our friend Lucy, a filmmaker who we recruit to join us for a week. When we first arrive at Noel's place, a big rambling house in the Lower Garden District, we walk in on a group of lesbians polishing off buckets of Popeyes chicken and glued to the TV, watching the drag king show they had just performed in. There is Noel on the screen, dancing onstage in guy's clothing. The women barely look up, but Noel, who is an old friend of one of my besties, jumps up and gives me a warm hug. Her bleached hair is shorn close to her head, and she's wearing baggy jeans and a muscle shirt. The last time I saw Noel she looked like a completely different person. She had long, angelic blond curls, wore tight jeans and lip gloss, and slept with guys. She was a ballerina and a flirt, the most stereotypically "feminine" woman ever. But now she looks happier, more comfortable, and more at ease with herself than I remember. I can't wait for the discussion that is coming, but for the moment, bed is all Emma and I can focus on.

The Loyola Ladies

On our first morning in New Orleans, we drive to Loyola University's tree-lined campus. Our first appointment is with Puja, a junior biology major minoring in business. Born and raised in New Orleans, Puja, twenty, is president of an on-campus group called Bridging the Gap, which promotes awareness of racial and cultural injustices by not "scolding people, but teaching them how to accept others." Puja doesn't call herself a feminist: "I'm defined as a woman, but that's not all I am. Being Hindu and raised in a Catholic city, Hinduism defines me more than being female." Puja feels connected to her cultural traditions, and she's "not completely against" arranged marriages because they are "based on compromises and family—everyone gets to be involved." When we touch on the topic of body image, Puja has a refreshingly positive point of view: "People becoming anorexic just to look like a movie star

> ## "Being Hindu and raised in a Catholic city, Hinduism defines me more than being female."
>
> —Puja

is really sad to me. I personally feel that I've never met an ugly person before. I believe that it is our duty as human beings to outweigh people's good qualities over their bad."

An hour later, we find a shady patch of grass with a couple of other young women. Maria is nineteen. Her family immigrated first to New Orleans and then to Kenner (just outside of New Orleans) from Nicaragua and moved to Miami after Hurricane Katrina. She's a sociology major who wants to travel after college and maybe become a human rights lawyer. Azebe, twenty-two, the daughter of Ethiopian immigrants, cites Katrina (or "the Storm," as many New Orleanians call it) as a major turning point in her life and wants to join Doctors Without Borders when she graduates.

They both consider themselves feminists. Maria says it's because she wants to be a "strong and independent person." Azebe simply explains, "I think I can accomplish anything." Both women are politically progressive and don't seem to put a box around the definition of feminism. Their views differ, though, when it comes to how feminism can conflict with traditional ideals. Maria tells us about her senior project assignment at her Catholic private high school—to plan out her own wedding. "I didn't like that people were

PUJA (TOP); MARIA (BOTTOM)

AZEBE

choosing my life for me," Maria says. "It scared me to think that women were taught that marriage was all there is—there's so much more!" But Azebe has a more personal interpretation of her faith, telling us, "Just because I'm a Christian doesn't mean I'm not a feminist. The way I see it, God wouldn't want women to waste their gifts."

Mayaba and Mandisa

Mayaba and Mandisa meet up with us in a café in Esplanade. The appointment is the end result of an exhausting struggle to find the voices of a particularly active group of women: those doing grass-roots, radically politicized work post Katrina. "I know a bunch of them," an old acquaintance told me, "but the thing is these women are so busy. They're busting their asses and they're hard to nail down." But after nagging and leaving messages all over town, we'd finally made a coffee date.

Our interview with Mayaba and Mandisa is short, but both women pack a punch in their bios. Mayaba, twenty-seven, works with INCITE!, the New Orleans Women's Health Clinic, and Critical Resistance, a grassroots organization whose work aims to expose the harm of what CR calls the prison industrial complex.

"The complex needs sexism, racism, classism, and heterosexism in place, or else people would realize that locking people up is not about safety, it's about money," Mayaba says. "In New Orleans, they're rebuilding a jail, and meanwhile kids aren't getting educated." Critical Resistance is now working on getting amnesty for prisoners whose cases were derailed or obscured by the destruction of Katrina.

Mandisa, twenty-two, moved to New Orleans from New York when she was ten. Through her work at INCITE!, she got involved with the Women's Health Clinic and the New Orleans Women's Health and Justice Initiative, and now is "a budding sexual health literacy organizer."

Mandisa worked in public housing in New Orleans when Katrina hit, which, she tells us, "got co-opted by white people. Public housing [inhabitants] in New Orleans were mostly black women and children. I have a serious problem with the white male taking the lead on this struggle. You can be an ally, but you can't just lead the movement."

INCITE!'s emphasis on the overlap of gender and race made Mandisa realize that "women of color are the ones who lie in this crazy intersection of vulnerability and violence." After the Storm, she found that people were talking plenty

"**Women of color
lie in this crazy
intersection of
vulnerability and
violence.**" —Mandisa

about race and class, but not about gender. "I saw myself on TV every day. I saw black women from the ages of five to fifty, yet there was no gender analysis of this storm. That was painful."

Mandisa describes the women involved in projects like the Health Clinic as "center[ing] the experiences of women of color in post-Katrina New Orleans and being committed to rendering ourselves visible." Mayaba adds, "When they shut down public housing, there was an 83 percent drop of female heads of households in New Orleans, mostly low-income, mostly black. Now the government is denying the fact that black women are back here, and they block federal grants and money to help this population. So the Women's Health Clinic is a point of resistance in itself, saying, 'Look, we're getting people in and providing these services . . . . There is a need.'"

Both women consider themselves feminists,

but not without qualifiers. "I identify as a queer black radical feminist," Mandisa says. "Feminism should not be devoid of race or ethnicity. Until we see that white supremacy and capitalism and patriarchy are all intertwined, then I question your gender politics." Mayaba agrees. "I'm a black radical feminist," she says. She was introduced to feminism through the white mainstream, and mentions Susan Faludi's *Backlash* as one of the first feminist texts she ever read. But most of it "left me stuck because it left race out of the picture." Adds Mayaba, "I'm not going to focus on forming feminism when we have this massive problem. Things are really oppressive right now."

Our interview nears an end when both ladies realize they need to leave shortly. As they rush out, one of Mandisa's earlier comments sticks in my mind: "I know a lot of people put a lot of emphasis on how we identify. But at the same time I'm just like, 'Fuck! Just do the work.'"

MAYABA (TOP); MANDISA (BOTTOM)

BATON ROUGE AND OUR FEMINIST FIESTA

J essica, who teaches digital media and graphic design at a high school in Baton Rouge, found us online through Feministing.com and invited us, via email, to a feminist dinner party in our honor. We arrive to find more than twenty women—teachers, attorneys, graduate students, activists, actresses, artists, bloggers. They form a tight-knit community, one that bands together in the conservative region by having forums, radio shows, and frequent soirees. The house is buzzing with politics and laughter, whether its occupants are chain-smoking around the campfire or eating cookies in the kitchen.

As we weave through the throngs, juicy tidbits of conversation fly off the walls. Two recent graduates tell us of being called "baby-killers" in the newspaper for working at Planned Parenthood, even though their branch doesn't even perform abortions—only one in Louisiana does. Another girl tells us about being drugged during the growing roofie problem on the LSU campus (fortunately, her friends got to her first).

These ladies are whip smart and ambitious, and they know how to turn their passions into action. Some are soon headed to Critical Sass, the women-friendly version of the popular bike march Critical Mass. A self-proclaimed 'triple threat' actress/singer/writer has just auditioned today for *Steel Magnolias*. Lucy finds herself in flirtation with a budding queer filmmaker who rules what New Orleanians call the "Hollywood of the South." Nona marvels at the turnout with our hostess Jessica.

When not chain-smoking and chatting by the campfire or guzzling instant refills of red wine, I am yelling "Who's ready for their mugshot?" and dragging the next victim into a corner for the camera flash.

Tonight, we learn that Baton Rouge has a badass feminist posse, full of dynamic women who hold their own amid a dearth of feminism in Louisiana, and that just a little blog could create a huge and delicious potluck. Our hostesses even let us pass out on their couch and in their guest room, and they offer breakfast in the morning. Talk about Southern hospitality.

—*Emma*

ALL THE BATON ROUGE LADIES

Noel

After dragging our hungover selves to our car and speeding back to New Orleans, we go out to lunch to finally interview Noel. She moved to the city a little less than two years ago to live with her mom, a native New Orleanian. Noel's mother had relocated to NOLA after her daughter's college graduation and had urged Noel to come down and do some work after Katrina. Noel worked for Common Ground for a while, establishing a media collective before turning to work for various non-profits and schools. Ultimately, she started doing video editing on a freelance basis. As for Noel's dramatic physical changes, she explains, "The process was slower than you think. I kinda knew I was gay when I went abroad to Stockholm and the girls were all free to be a little bi. Then I took a look at Loren Cameron's *Body Alchemy* [a book of transsexual portraits]. At first I thought, *Hmm, that's kinda sexy*, then *No, this is too alternative, too weird*. But eventually I ended up dating a trans male for nine months."

NOEL

Noel describes her straight life as having been unnerving for years. "I don't know why, but I felt like I had to be the girliest girl. Other girls weren't very nice to me, and guys were just ridiculous. I felt like I wasn't well-respected and faced the most absurd amount of harassment. I even had gender nightmares. I made drastic changes to make my experience as a woman better. Being with women feels so much better for me." Noel does connect her sexuality with feminism but notes that she was a feminist from the start. "My mom was a huge tomboy, and I had elements of that, too. When I dated guys, I always wanted to take on some masculine traits and be one of the guys, and they just weren't into it."

She sees straight guys, out of everyone, as the most stuck in the gender binary. "If a guy hooks up with a guy, it's epic, but with girls, it's more accepted. People are progressing, but so far it's just little pockets." To Noel, the future of feminism includes expanding definitions of gender. "I really like the fact that in the queer community, gender-bending is an actual activity, like our drag show. It's just inefficient and unintuitive to separate genders." Noel later tells us how at this point in her life she feels "mostly attracted to idea of androgyny, [because] only allowing one set of traits to show puts you into a very narrow corner. I also value equality in my relationships, because I don't want either of us to have to be the 'girl' and hold less social validity in comparison to the partner."

Lynn

After a couple hours of strolling around in the Marigny, we get to our date with Lynn. She looks like a punked-out Baby Spice, sporting high orange pigtails and tattoos dotting her chest and arms. The centerpiece, right below her neckline, is an elaborate illustration of the Little Prince, stars and all, with an inscription from the book peeking out: "All those things you tame you become responsible for forever." A self-proclaimed "Army brat," Lynn, twenty-five, has gotten around but considers New Orleans her home. She feels such a connection to the city that she abandoned her full scholarship to college in Philly because she hated the East Coast so much. "I was a weird kid because I actually talked to people and looked them in the eye," Lynn says.

Lynn became a feminist in her early teens. "My parents started telling me to look for a husband in eighth grade," she confesses. "They told me that college is a waste of money for a woman because I should be a wife and mother." Feminism made sense to Lynn when she was told that she would be kicked out of her own home if she went to college, simply because she was a woman. After Katrina, her sense of being a woman became even stronger. "At one point, there was one woman for every twenty-five men, and everyone tried to grope you [on the streets]. There was an extreme intensity in the air."

Lynn's live-in-the-moment, plan-phobic attitude also coalesced after Katrina. After the Storm, she said, "locals realized that there was a big bad world out there. I gave up on the planning, because if you can't take joy in the moment, then why would you bother?" On her goals for the future, though, she's clear: "If I had one life goal, it would be working in sex education and sexual health."

Lynn gets to talking about her two jobs—being a bartender at a Hustler strip club on Bourbon Street and a saleswoman at a sex toy shop. "Sex work is an inherently feminist act," she proclaims. "Working voluntarily in the sex industry is lessening the gender dichotomy and reclaiming something that patriarchy has made us feel shameful about." She tells us that most women at her club love what they do. Lynn sees burlesque troupes like Big Star in Austin or alt-porn sites like SuicideGirls as no more or less feminist than mainstream strip clubs and porn. "The industry has really high standards, very regulated. Also, a lot of women are turned on by mainstream porn!" She also describes the everyday

LYNN

triumphs of working at the sex shop, telling us about how just the other day she enlightened a sixty-year-old woman about her orgasmic clitoris.

Imagine our surprise, then, when Lynn suddenly says, "Feminists are such in a rush to be inclusive that they try make too many things fit within the feminist movement. Sex really shouldn't be so important." But didn't we just spend the last forty-five minutes talking about Lynn's sex-positive attitude, how stripping is a feminist act, how women should know how to give themselves an orgasm? Slipping out of "interviewer" mode, I practically get in a full-blown argument with her. I feel almost insulted that she would brush sex to the side like that. It reminds me of how Betty Friedan, one of the most important feminist voices in history, dismissed sex drive and conversations about it by claiming that it actually hurt the Women's Movement. Was Lynn, prostripping bartender extraordinaire, saying the same thing?

"I think we get mired into these interesting discussions about sex, and at the same time lose sight of other changes," explains Lynn.

"What about the sixty-year-old woman?" I protest.

Lynn stands her ground. "Talking about sex is treating the symptoms and not the disease. Until we change society's views, we will still have to be teaching sixty-year-old women how to get off."

Lynn decides to give us the walking tour of

> ## "Working voluntarily in the sex industry is reclaiming something that patriarchy has made us feel shameful about." —Lynn

the Marigny area we have just lunched in. The air is surprisingly chilly for autumn in Louisiana, and Emma is in photographic awe of the decaying Gothic Southern mansions and overgrown vines lining the avenues. Lynn takes us to an old, deserted estate, its cracked windows matching the macabre mood of the district. Emma insists that Lucy put down her video camera as she notices that her rosy British look matches the crumbling pink doorstep she is standing on. She seems to be a ghost in a vintage photograph as soon as the shutter is clicked.

The aura of New Orleans is truly unnerving, and we are starting to understand why Lynn noted, "We consider ourselves the farthest north point of the Caribbean." The bright hues of the row houses are only matched by the confrontational, colorful characters who inhabit them.

LUCY

THE STREET URCHINS

We are stopped by a fierce girl on a bicycle wearing a bundle of crumpled dollar bills safety-pinned to her collar. "Wanna give me a dollar?" she asks.

We all look down, embarrassed, not knowing how to respond. "See, you must be from out of town, if you don't know the New Orleans tradition of giving someone a dollar on their birthday."

An equally odd character approaches, interrupting the awkward moment by issuing a "Hey, Charlotte." The scene must be small here. Angie, whom we later dub the "street urchin," looks like she has stepped out of a 1930s train-traveling troupe. She tells us she plays in a bluegrass band, and refuses to give her age—"I don't believe in ages"—but looks about twelve. We get their take on feminism:

Charlotte: "I know we're the ones to bring people into this crap-ass world. I know I'm a woman, but I like to keep things PG. When people talk about their vaginas, I'm like errrr . . . "

Angie: "I don't know if I'm a feminist. I believe in equality."

ANGIE

CHARLOTTE

THE FRENCH QUARTER

Our night is a mirage of oil-lit lamps on cobblestone streets, breast-shaped red lights flashing, white columns lit by the moonlight, and doors swinging open on their own. New Orleans is a striking mixture of American folklore and sleaze.

After a dinner of étouffée and mint juleps, we go for a stroll down Bourbon Street. We pass the Hustler club that Lynn works at and even see Mayaba out of the corner of our eye. New Orleans is a small town. We walk around arm in arm, in a silent rapture, stumbling to avoid groups of heckling frat boys and sloppy stiletto heels. We try to approach it all with a "When in Rome" attitude, but the smell of cheap flavored vodka in hot pink plastic rattles our nostrils and the rousing shouts for ladies fall rough on our ears. Nona and I agree: "This is sleazier than Vegas!"

I start to feel guilty for being judgmental. Has feminism made us "no fun"? At first, I fear that we have become too self-aware and serious to get down with some good old-fashioned piña colada-infused bump and grind. But then I remember the concept of false consciousness: the natural habitat of Girls Gone Wild just seems full of wasted women who don't quite know why they are having fun.

We drive the long route back to Noel's, slowly crawling through the ghostly Garden District with the whispery sounds of Blonde Redhead floating from our car radio. We fantasize that every enclosed porch holds a secret, every swinging screen door an invisible past. As we all three curl into the same small bed, I lie awake with the taste of tonight on my tongue. This whole city is haunted with history, tainted by taboo. It is spicy and shadowy all at once. But nothing seems to lift the sadness of the storm, which clings to every shattered window and broken tree branch.

—Emma

THE iRoN RAIL

owhere is this post-apocalyptic flavor better embodied than at our next stop, where we find Kate perched at nightfall on her fire escape of the industrial loft, also home to the anarchist bookstore and arts space the Iron Rail . . .

The bookstore overflows with literature, zines, records, and attractive gutter punks . . .

Sarah, a trapeze artist, invites us to join the evening's free yoga class . . .

Kate

Finally, we head up to Kate's loft, a sprawling open space filled with wall murals, vintage couches, and fogged factory windows. While brewing tea, we take turns on the swing that hangs from the ceiling beams.

Kate tells us she had a feminist upbringing in Phoenix, but chooses "not to identify with that label anymore. Anarchist is a more powerful label. It means fighting all hierarchies." Kate, twenty-seven, became frustrated with the male-dominated anarchist movement some years back, but after attending the North American Anarchist conference in 2000 in Los Angeles, she became inspired by the presence of "loud, brash anarchist women" and decided to make a documentary called *The Anarcha Project* to provide a forum for the voices of female and trans anarchists. So far she has video-interviewed over two hundred people and is still working with the hopes it will become "an interview compilation, sort of a library resource."

We inch forward to hear Kate over the loud soundtrack her roommates have been pumping, a constant lullaby of the Cranberries, CoCoRosie, Clipse, the Knife, and Townes Van Zandt. Our eyes widen as they play songs that have been in constant rotation in our car stereo. I whisper to Nona "I can't believe this! It must be fate!" This is a charmed night.

Despite her continued involvement in anarchist action, Kate tells us she became frustrated with the stagnancy of rhetoric and decided to push her interest in women's health and social justice into a career as a midwife. She tells us about a pivotal moment when she attended a birth the night before Katrina hit. "Before, I politically analyzed every situation. Now I am more in touch with exhibiting compassion, using my hands. [In midwifery], I've found an outlet for my liberation politics—attending births and helping at the hospital, increasing patient info, giving power back to the mother." Kate previously worked at a national reproductive health nonprofit, but found it "disempowering": "There was a desperation for professionalism and acceptance of the status quo. Many feminists automatically assume that if someone gets pregnant at a young age, they're not going to have any kind of life. It's a weak analysis around gender combined with an undercurrent of racism and classism."

—*Emma*

KATE

AcRoSS THe CaNaL

The next morning we pack our belongings into the car, en route to Memphis, with one final stop. We can't leave the city without heading to the site of the most intense Katrina destruction, the Ninth Ward. We are hesitant about being disaster tourists—I keep remembering my disgust for Ground Zero tourists in New York. "Never Forget" felt like a tagline for selling sentimentality and false pride to eager suburbanites. But this morning, we became those outsiders, dying to find the most horrifying material proof that this storm had really happened.

I jump out of the car every few minutes while Nona drives behind me. I must photograph every little gory piece of evidence. Over two years later, we are traveling through a wreckage that looks untouched, except for crude spray paint markings on houses that have been cleared for dead dogs or deadly odors.

As we stumble upon a smattering of inhabited streets, Lucy and I begin to feel shame for using our cameras to invade what now seems a sacred piece of private sanity for those brave enough to return. We feel our skin shining like a bright, evil, white light, contaminating our otherwise innocent effort with the ever-present race tensions that this hurricane represents. Nona disagrees. "The only way to educate ourselves is to look out the window and see it for ourselves. Look." She points to a husky black man with a camcorder. "That guy is filming, too. We can't ignore this forever."

But I can't shake this sense of guilt. My camera suddenly seems like a violent weapon. After five weeks, I felt for the first time like

we were looking at and not with. I want to hand over my camera to the young boy playing in a heap of garbage. What right do I have to document his struggle?

These are the contradictions of our shared American identity. This is the reason to go on the road. To face the possible falsity of finding one national character. But our compassion is real. Whether it be New Orleans or New Delhi, this is a human catastrophe, one that is clearly contained in every boarded up window we pass.

The eerie character of New Orleans suddenly becomes less a fairytale of magical phantoms and more a morbid reminder of broken political promises. This is not the ghost town located in our collective Disney consciousness. Suddenly tangible is a haunted American history less charmed, one of lynching trees rather than rusty saloon doors. It is time for us to move on to our next stop, but this is something we will, for better or worse, Never Forget.

—*Emma*

CHAPTER 9 - - **Walking the Line** - - →

MEMPHIS

Our first night in Memphis is our friend Lucy's last, and we are sad to lose not only her unique perspective but also her incredibly keen sense of direction. But for the moment, even the directions on our BlackBerry can't guide us through the twisty-turny section of Memphis where our hostess and next interviewee, Krista, lives. After ending up in several dead ends, we call Krista in desperation. Much to our relief, she guides the three of us to a warmly bustling bar. With the promise of live music later on at the famed Hi-Tone, where we're meeting up with a musician Emma saw play in Chicago a few months back, we settle into our now-familiar routine.

Krista

Originally from Sioux Falls, South Dakota, Krista moved to the city after she got a job teaching high school biology in North Memphis. She doesn't consider herself a feminist because "calling one-self a feminist is an excuse for bad behavior." She explains, "A lot of feminists I know tend to be anti-man and anti-trans. They gloss over things like race and class. I took one class on feminism in college and found that there was a lot missing, so I decided to study rocks instead."

As a teacher, she does notice gender issues forming early on: "Girls in the high school where I teach either act cute and dumb, or tough—that's how they deal with things. They will hide the strong, intelligent part of themselves in front of boys."

Alicja

We meet Alicja at HiTone, the eclectic retro-style rock club Krista has brought us to. She's tending door tonight, but Alicja is singer and guitarist for an array of Memphis-based bands, including the Lost Sounds and the River City Tanlines. I saw Alicja play in Chicago when she was six months pregnant and rocking out in a flowing red dress, riling up the crowd with her punk pregnancy per-formance. On a break between sets, she pulls us into the back room for a chat, before shooing us back to see the bands at a special discount. She

is clearly a fixture in the scene here, as every few moments our interview is interrupted by a hello or congratulations on her new baby. Alicja tells us she started playing music with girls in high school, but always related more to males in rock music.

Has she experienced any discrimination being a woman in the male-dominated garage and punk scenes? She looks bored with the question, but lets us know "men always soundcheck you last, look embarrassed for you, and try to give advice to you if you are in an all-girl band." She tells us that she hopes her newborn daughter will be impressed with her mom one day, that she'll see her with a "flying v-guitar" and think "mom is a bad-ass."

Does she relate to feminism? "I secretly get satisfaction from the feminist movement, but I have felt repelled by the term and by women who can't stand up for themselves without relating to the term. I know I am a great guitarist already." Alicja's attitude is typical of many woman who have traded irreverence and confidence for being pigeonholed. "I can't live down the stereotype of always being a woman in rock. I don't under-stand—women are not a race. We are not like the Aztecs or Eskimos. We are 50 percent of the world. Why do we keep being defined as separate from it?"

—*Emma*

ALICJA (TOP); KRISTA (BOTTOM)

NASHVILLE

After dropping off Lucy at the airport, we drive to Caroline's house in Nashville, Tennessee, but not before cruising down a street full of honky-tonks—all bumpin', all free. Unlike Memphis, the music menu at these bars isn't varied. This town is straight country and damn proud of it. We can't resist popping into a cobbler's shop and scoring some cowboy boots; by some miracle, I rustle up a pair of amazing white, fringed boots in the sale-of-sales bin. There's no question: The city's mood is infectious, and we can't wait to talk to the women who inhabit this place.

Rachel

We have coffee in a hipster part of Nashville with Rachel, the twenty-four-year-old art and design director at *American Songwriter* magazine. She grew up in Memphis, where she and her two sisters were raised by Southern Baptist parents. "My parents are conservative but always gave us freedom as to how we approached our talents. I grew up with the arts," Rachel says. She came to Nashville "to do music—I was fascinated with how the DIY independent music scene was going in Nashville." But then she wound up getting a business degree and eventually became interested in design.

Rachel would consider herself a feminist, but "subtly," she says. "It's in my nature to feel empowered as a female. I always feel like I have to prove myself, even in the independent music scene, which I see as kind of a brotherhood." Rachel describes herself as "quiet shaker." She cites her parents as unlikely contributors to her progressive way of thinking. "My parents are both religious people, but they're all about freedom of speech. My mom grew up in the hippie culture in Austin, although she describes that time in her life as 'before she found her faith.'" Regardless, Rachel and her two older sisters "honed in" on their parents' liberal past rather than the more traditional lifestyle they gravitated toward later on.

Religion does play a role in Rachel's life. "It's

RACHEL

a very quiet factor, but I treasure it," she tells us. The church she goes to "embraces the concept of love between races and all types of people," and goes against the stereotype of closed-minded Christianity. She thinks her anti-right-wing stance and the fact that she is pro-choice, is "even more powerful because I am a Christian. It surprises people. I also get excited when I meet people who are both faithful and artists—because I sometimes feel like an outcast in either group." Rachel feels adamant about the importance of separation between church and state and gets frustrated that the right-wing agenda uses the name of Christ.

Rachel is hopeful for the future of young women and is eager for them to be included in what she calls the creative class. "I get encouraged when I find that needle in a haystack—a woman who is pursuing the male-dominated world of music or art. I think it's getting better. People are finally allowing people to think for themselves and, little by little, boundaries are vanishing."

Caroline

Caroline, twenty-six, is my back-in-the-day friend from Wesleyan. Raised in Montclair, New Jersey, she has been in Nashville for three years getting her medical degree at Vanderbilt. Over a Thai dinner, Caroline tells us that she absolutely considers herself a feminist. "It's something about

myself that I have known since I was young," she says. Caroline describes her family as a "feminist household," crediting both her mom and her dad for raising her that way. Her mother, who is a teacher, regrets not getting professional training until her late thirties, so it was important to her for her children to have real careers. "Both me and my sister are off-the-beaten-path kind of people, but we are both in professional schools, and that's not an accident. My mom wanted us to be able to support ourselves."

A couple years ago, Caroline had told me she wanted to be an ob/gyn, but has since changed her mind. "The way women are treated, it is so impersonal and cold. There's a whole atmosphere of talking about the women like they're annoying, speaking of them in very negative ways. It's not geared to help women through the birth process."

Emma, fresh with thoughts on midwifery from our interview with Kate in New Orleans, asks how homeopathic and natural procedures are dealt with in medical school. "The institution doesn't teach it, but I see value in it," Caroline replies. "I'm just trying to get everything I can out of my medical education, so I can make it more holistic in the future." I make the instant parallel between Caroline and a feminist who thinks, "If you can't beat 'em, join 'em, then use the knowledge to beat 'em later." It is an age-old feminist tactic for a woman to go along with the system until she gains a certain amount of power and *then* to change things.

Caroline wants to be successful, but she wants to "live like a human." In many aspects of the medical field, she says, "you have to sacrifice your family for your career, like with surgeons. I want a life outside of medicine. I like the idea of doing home visits or healthcare in the public schools or in community centers. You can achieve much more by considering a person's health in the context of their family situation or their home or school environment."

"Is that why fewer women are surgeons?" I ask. "Probably, because they are less willing to be in a chauvinistic, hierarchical environment," she replies. And it may not be just that women are softer, but more that "there's been a slow change in our culture where you can't just boss everyone around. I don't see myself setting the world on fire, but I see me and my peers collectively changing medical education and the practice of medicine over time."

MUSIC SCENE

Memphis and Nashville, as expected, are vibrating with music.

At our night at the Hi-Tone, we listen to bluegrass, soul, country and dirty-South hip-hop, all for five dollars.

At Graceland, the tour vans are packed full of tourists eager to touch their fingertips to Elvis's stairway.

Caroline brings us to Broadway for beers and a session at the honky-tonk.

We feel perfectly at home in our newly acquired, authentic Nashville cowboy boots.

HI TONE MEMPHIS .COM
10-6 KING BISCUIT
10-7 FLUFF GIRL
10-8 DJ SPOOKY
10-9 BURY THE LIVING

Lauren

After visiting a few honky-tonks with Caroline, we rush to meet Lauren, another med student at Vanderbilt. Lauren, twenty-three, grew up in Memphis, went to nursing school in Texas, and just moved to Nashville in April to get her master's in midwifery. Lauren echoes some of Caroline's hesitance about current ob/gyn protocol, telling us, "Women are often treated like machines." She believes that the birthing process is a woman's domain. "I don't think there's room for men in child-birthing. It makes things awkward when a male doctor enters, even though I do respect some male doctors. Midwives really believe in women's bodies and that women can do it on their own."

Does Lauren consider herself a feminist? "I wouldn't. I don't have the clearest picture of what it truly is, but I have a definite need for men in my life. When I was getting into midwifery, I heard stories about feminists that are very anti-men, antiestablishment, 'hear us roar.' That's not my heart. From what I know of it, feminism seems like an imbalance. But I do think women were created beautifully and created strong, and I want women to be able to fulfill that, even in childbirth."

LAUREN

> "I think women were created beautifully and created strong, and I want women to be able to fulfill that, even in childbirth."
>
> —Lauren

We ask her if there are any other issues she is passionate about. "Yes," she says. "Abortion. I'm very pro-life. I believe that every pregnancy is a gift from the Lord and that there is a life at the moment of conception. I volunteer at a Crisis Pregnancy Center, and I've worked with women who have had abortions who feel like they have killed someone. I also see the lack of counseling given to pregnant women. I know women have their own choices, but I don't think they know about the other options out there." Lauren concedes that if abortion were illegal, "there will be some women that will abort no matter what, so more women's lives would be at risk."

Lauren's pro-life stance is directly related to her faith, which is extremely important to her. Unlike Rachel, the separation of church and state "is really hard for me," she tells us. "My relationship with the Lord is everything in my life. I don't ever want to live a compartmentalized life; I strive to be the same person wherever I am." Lauren sees the Christian right's agenda as compatible with her views on women. "I don't think President Bush is perfect by any means, and he professes to be a Christian. No matter how good a person is, they are going to make mistakes. But I believe Jesus supports women 100 percent."

"Do pro-life male politicians have a place in legislating abortion if they don't have a place in the delivery room?" I ask. "My gut instinct is yes," she answers. "Their position of being pro-life furthers knowledge and education, instead of them just wanting to have control of women."

Lauren is concerned that too many young women "play around with sex," and she believes in waiting to have sex until she is married. "I'm a virgin myself," she tells us. "I grew up in a high school where most of my friends dated guys, and I was the girl they came to, crushed, after they broke up with them. The girls were just giving themselves away. They were getting broken and torn apart. When I finally do get married, I want to be whole and not have had my heart broken." But if Lauren were to counsel a young woman on sex, "I'd maybe tell my own story, tell them about the risks, but I would also give them birth control." Lauren doesn't believe in abstinence-only education "because it's

not a reality. Girls need to know about STDs and pregnancy." With both premarital sex and abortion, Lauren's goal is "not to change or judge people, but to accept people, counsel them and give them advice. If a sixteen-year-old girl comes to me and decides to go through with an abortion, I will still support her."

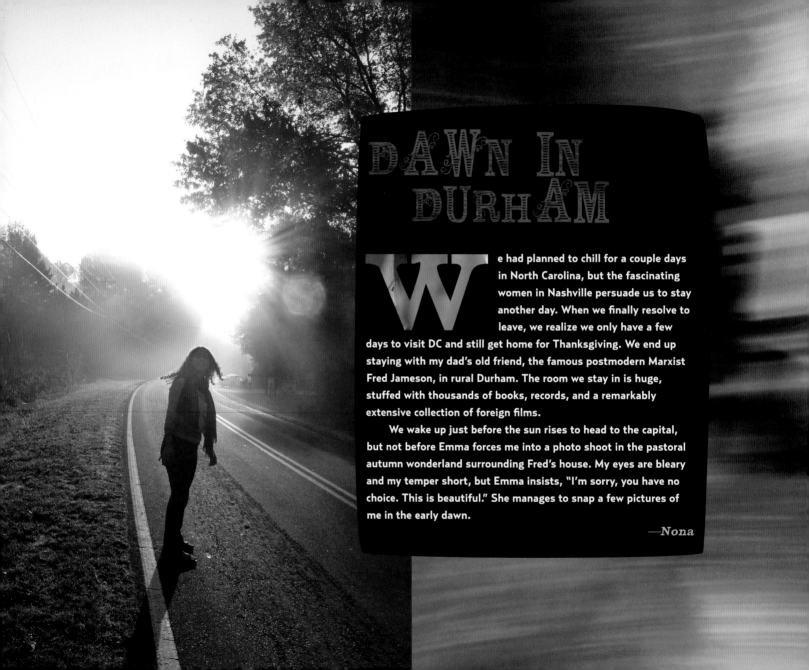

DAWN IN DURHAM

We had planned to chill for a couple days in North Carolina, but the fascinating women in Nashville persuade us to stay another day. When we finally resolve to leave, we realize we only have a few days to visit DC and still get home for Thanksgiving. We end up staying with my dad's old friend, the famous postmodern Marxist Fred Jameson, in rural Durham. The room we stay in is huge, stuffed with thousands of books, records, and a remarkably extensive collection of foreign films.

We wake up just before the sun rises to head to the capital, but not before Emma forces me into a photo shoot in the pastoral autumn wonderland surrounding Fred's house. My eyes are bleary and my temper short, but Emma insists, "I'm sorry, you have no choice. This is beautiful." She manages to snap a few pictures of me in the early dawn.

—Nona

WASHINGTON, DC

Because of our Nashville dilly-dallying, we have time for only one quick-and-dirty interview in DC before we head home. Despite the fall weather, it is unseasonably hot—everyone on the Mall is in their T-shirts and flats. Even the flowers at the Botanic Garden, the site of our lunch date, are still fully in bloom. The eerily warm weather seems a perfect condition to talk to our next environmentally conscious interviewees—two staffers for the Energy and Commerce Committee on Capitol Hill.

Melissa and Rachel

Rachel and Melissa have only a few minutes to talk on their lunch break. Rachel is a twenty-four-year-old legislative clerk from the New York area who moved here right after graduation. She studied earth and environmental sciences and wants to use her science to make a "bigger difference." She eventually wants to be an environmental attorney. Melissa grew up in Bethesda, Maryland, works in the health department of the committee, and comes from a long line of politicos. Being involved in politics seemed like a natural step for her.

Rachel is a feminist because she is "proud to be a woman." Melissa agrees that women can do everything guys can do. Both are sensitive to women's issues. Rachel says coming to DC at the tail end of a conservative administration has meant seeing how those values bleed into professional settings. She notes, "Women and minorities need more advanced degrees in this town. If you're a white man, it doesn't seem to matter as much. It's a pretty traditional place."

Melissa nods, pointing out that much of DC is based on old-school connections. "I got my job through my dad's network," she tells us. "Women are definitely at a disadvantage in terms of networking."

"Yes!" Rachel says excitedly. "But sometimes it's hard to build that network when women are petty toward each other." Rachel cites "cattiness" among women as a major obstacle to women's advancement in the workplace. "Hello, we need to be a team here!" she exclaims. Melissa tells us that she felt this exact vibe at her former job. "I felt like the women I worked with were very focused on their own agendas."

We're curious about the issues on these ladies' minds, and Melissa has an immediate answer. "We've been trying to kill abstinence-only programs. It really prevents people from learning

MELISSA

> **"Women and minorities need more advanced degrees in this town. If you're a** white man, it doesn't seem to matter **as much."**
>
> **—Rachel**

about safe sexual practices." She tells us she gets irritated when pro-life women use the fact that they're women themselves—therefore they "know better"—just to push the abstinence-only agenda. She points out that this cuts across party lines, noting that she feels Hillary uses the pure fact of her gender in a manipulative way.

Rachel says she'd like to see people tackle the work/life balance more aggressively. "Professional women should be able to have a career and a good family. It should all be easier!" she says. "Especially around here, it seems impossible. You always have to be on call, work late. The political scene is a really demanding culture."

RACHEL

CHAPTER 10 --- **Bringing It All Back Home** --->

NEW YORK CITY

We are greeted by our native city with unfathomable Thanksgiving traffic. Instead of relief rushing in, madness takes its place as we sit in Upper West Side gridlock, remembering why we wanted to escape New York in the first place. Finally, I get Emma home and I begin the drive back to my father's house in Jackson Heights. I feel more tired than I ever have in my life, but one glance at the schedule for the next two weeks reminds me that I need to keep it together for what seems like the millions of New York interviews we've booked. We seriously have some work to do.

Kathleen

Kathleen Hanna is an activist, teacher, and musician; an early Riot Grrrl upstarter and to some the emblem of the '90s feminist revival; singer/songwriter in Viva Knievel, Bikini Kill, Julie Ruin, and Le Tigre; and above all, Emma's personal she-ro. Emma had written gushing fan letters to Kathleen during her Riot Grrrl days—and, to her surprise, got a postcard back. To Emma, Kathleen was the kind of icon that remained completely accessible to her young female fans.

When we meet with her in a tiny café near NYU, Kathleen tells us about how she got her start as a musician: "I had been writing things that I stuffed in my bottom drawer and didn't let anybody see—not very linear, but I knew it was passionate." Later, in Seattle, she met feminist novelist and poet Kathy Acker, who asked her why she wanted to write. When Kathleen responded by saying she didn't think anybody listened to her, Kathy said, "Why are you doing spoken word? No one goes to spoken word. You should start a band." So she went back to Olympia, and that's what she did. "It was just one of those life-changing moments," she tells us.

Kathleen is now going to school at NYU for design. "I just got really sick of music," she says. But she originally chose music as a medium because it made it a lot easier "to be the Pied Piper of feminism. It creates both false and real

senses of community." She admits that at first, the formation of a girl-friendly punk scene was more out of necessity than altruism. "Bikini Kill [Kathleen's band] was a total shit magnet. Living in a small town and being a total fucking loudmouth punk rocker is not as fun as you might think. Our shows were incredibly violent and really scary. We needed to play with like-minded bands; it's really hard to go onstage when a guy is calling you 'riot bitch' in your face backstage."

Pretty soon, though, the "feminist" part became deliberate. "I lived in the '90s, when *Time* and *Newsweek* came out in the same couple months with covers announcing feminism was dead," Kathleen remembers. "This was right when I was having my moment with all my girlfriends of, 'Omigod, feminism is real, it is changing our lives,' and right then those magazines came out. And I was like, 'I gotta tell everyone it's alive in Olympia, my friends, we're all doing it!' I was like an evangelical, I was! I was a little feminist preacher."

Eventually, Kathleen separated herself from the Riot Grrrl movement because of "the weird lefty-guilt bullshit" that often happens when social activists fight among themselves and that happened when

KATHLEEN

Second Wave feminists viciously criticized each other. Not that she has abandoned feminism. It was more the complete faith in the concept that was the problem. "When the thing that totally saved your life is now choking you to death, the language that saved your life is now being used to murder you, it's really incredibly painful." But "it's the arrogance of youth that made anything happen. I am glad I opened my mouth even though I didn't fully know what I was saying."

We are so into hearing about the rise and fall of Riot Grrrl, and the feminist in-fighting, that we almost forget to ask Kathleen our main question: What does she hope young feminists will tackle? "I hope you take on the psychological dimensions of activism and the pitfalls of it. How do you tell the difference between horizontal oppression and productive dialogue that is difficult to hear?"

MARISOL

> ## "How do you tell the difference between horizontal oppression and *productive dialogue* that is difficult to hear? —Kathleen

Kathleen wants women to learn who they are as activists, and after butting their heads against some of the same problems of the past, "they will hopefully survive on the other end and be able to move forward." We are amazed. We feel like Kathleen has eavesdropped on one of our long car ride conversations. What she hopes is what we've been talking about—that this half-forgotten history learned from our mothers and mentors does not discourage us; that it instead pushes us forward to talk to our generation—productively.

Marisol

We are lost in the windings of the cobblestoned Financial District, hopelessly trying to find Marisol's office. Finally, bubbly Marisol materializes and beckons us to a sushi spot. It's been over a year since I've seen her. She was on the swim team with me in high school. Marisol is twenty-two, born to a Puerto Rican mom and an Austrian dad. She has always been a perfectionist and admits to having the "first-generation drive of succeeding, whatever that means." For Marisol, it meant getting into Yale and becoming an analyst at one of the biggest and most well-known investment banking firms in the world.

But money isn't as important to her as she thought. "I grew up having no money, and I was always thinking that life will be so much easier if I have it. It actually doesn't make much of a difference." She is shifting gears next fall, trying for her postbaccalaureate degree at Columbia. "I was trying to find a job where I had a lot of options," she explains, "but what I realize is that there's this corporate culture, the same dynamic of how you get from one place to another, and that's just not the life I want to have."

Our minds have been on one track for months, so we ask if this decision has anything to do with the gender dynamics of the firm. "No," Marisol says. "Not at all." To Marisol's surprise, "investment banks in New York are very modern in terms of women, childcare, minorities, diversity—they have it down." And it's not that she thinks these banks act out of the goodness of their feminist hearts. "It's just smart," she concludes. "They realize that to work in the modern world and to get the best types of people you have to provide certain services and environments, otherwise you're going to lose women. There are three women in my group who recently had children, and the company provides a childcare center in the building. That's a lot better than other industries with more women." Still, she emphasizes that this is very different from the rest of American corporations, like GM or AT&T. "These banks are five years ahead," she asserts.

Michele

"Young women are concerned about effectiveness and concerned about making things happen, and yet they don't want to be identified as feminists," Michele Wallace declares before our first question is even uttered. *Tell me about it,* I say to myself. Michele reclines in her office chair, deep in thought, and continues to offer her twisty-turny analysis. She is a New York–born feminist, author, cultural critic, and professor of English at City College and the CUNY Graduate Center. She is also one of my longtime idols, ever since my mom handed me Michele's book, *Black Macho and the Myth of the Superwoman,* in which she unapologetically calls out the sexism of black nationalists.

> "**Young women are concerned about making things happen, and yet they don't want to be** identified as feminists." —**Michele**

MICHELE

Michele is the daughter of famed feminist artist Faith Ringgold and admits that her mom was one of her first feminist influences—though the relationship was not without some tension between them that was essential to her feminism. "I began to break with my mother when *Black Macho* came out. She felt as though I was ripping her off and not giving her adequate credit, but I was encouraged to leave my mother behind, as many feminists were. There was general hostility and suspicion toward mothers." This is why Michele was interested in *Girldrive*, which she repeatedly tells us has touched her in a big way. The project is framed by the connection with our mothers—"hearing and writing about other people's voices," is the way she puts it. She tells us that rebellion toward moms was much more integral to feminism when she was younger.

We ask her about the future. Being a professor, she keeps coming back to one idea: education. She says, "College is a major agent of dissemination for feminist ideas. When I was a teenager, I saw a lot of activity in terms of feminism with my mother and activists in New York, but if it had not been backed up by one of the first women's studies programs here in City College, I don't know what it would have meant for me." In school, Michele read women writers and witnessed the struggle of the women faculty in her college. She doesn't deem a college education necessary in activist cities like New York, but outside of political hubs, "the academic part of it is even more important."

Erica

I have a nasty cold the day of our meeting with Erica Jong, which annoys me to no end. I've admired her ever since I was writing my thesis about porn and the sexual revolution, and I was looking forward to having an animated discussion.

ERICA

Instead, I'm all snotty and groggy, armed with Ricola and Puffs, but I try to keep it together as we interview Erica in her to-die-for Upper East Side apartment.

Erica Jong is a native New Yorker, a writer and poet most famous for her sexually bold and then-shocking first novel, *Fear of Flying*. The book was published in 1973, in the thick of an era of sexual liberation and defiance that was, depending on who you ask, instrumental in defining Second Wave feminism.

I ask Erica about women's reactions to *Flying*'s sexually free protagonist, Isadora. She admits she had no idea the book would be such a big deal. Many reviewers were vicious and scathing. "But from normal women," she tells us, "the most frequent response was, 'I thought I was crazy; you've made me feel less lonely, like I'm not a freak.' For them, it signified the new sexual freedom."

Naturally, Emma and I are curious to hear Erica's take on the sexual revolution's legacy—the emotional minefield of the so-called "hookup culture." She answers that it depends. "Is experimentation something that makes you feel threatened and insecure, or is it something you can enjoy and learn from? The taboos aren't there anymore, but a lot of women find themselves feeling very insecure, unloved, and taken for granted." Yes, yes, we know. But why? we press. Why do women have such a hard time with this?

She continues, "What we've asked women to do, which is so damn hard, is to make their own rules based on their emotional needs—and at such an early age! Being completely free is more than what some unformed young women can deal with."

"Yeah," I sigh wistfully.

"Some women wish that we could go back to formal dating—at least you'd know what to expect!" Emma jokes.

Erica declares that all teenage girls need an older woman to talk about promiscuity, love, and sex. "Maybe not our mothers, since we are all rebelling against her at that age—but someone who she trusts. Maybe every woman ought to have a mentor."

I start to have an epiphany. Why don't we talk more often about sex with older women who've been through it all? It's logical that we wouldn't rely on our mothers when it comes to the confusions of sex—as Michele had told us, railing against one's mother is a rite of passage. Plus, who talks about sex with her *mom*? Still, Erica was right: "Unformed" fourteen-year-old girls bear the burden of making the exact right choices about sex all on their own. Even the best sex ed doesn't have a unit on emotions. "Mentoring is the new feminism," Erica concludes. "I really believe that the next stage of feminism is going to be younger women and older women working together."

With that, Erica fixes me a hot Emergen-C, loads me up with tissues, and sends us on our way.

NEW YORK ODYSSEYS

Being New York City natives is a blessing and a curse—our connections spread far and wide, but that means our Christmas vacation consists of trekking up and down and across and back through the MTA, scrambling to our next appointment in bone-chilling slush, smooshed up against Christmas tourists for subway stops on end. On these pages is a mere sampling of where we ventured to in order to get a sense of New Yorkers' feelings about feminism.

TECLA, *TWENTY-FIVE, SOUTH BRONX*

PIA D., *TWENTY-THREE, UPPER EAST SIDE*

Native New Yorker, preschool teacher, plays keyboard and does backup vocals in the all-girl band SwEEtie, feminist.

New Yorker, occasional dancer, socially conscious entrepreneur, just finished an internship with the Clinton Foundation. Has never thought about it, but when asked, considers herself a feminist.

"I like having that beautiful female vibe without having to deal with male energy. I know that women have their own issues with each other, but being with girl musicians feels like a more healthy, cohesive environment, where you can vibe in a pleasant way."

"I'm a feminist in the business sense. I'm getting my real estate degree to be able to make some money and start my first company without any help from anyone. I'm sick of living from paycheck to paycheck."

RYAN, *TWENTY-SIX, EAST VILLAGE*

Born and raised in Queens, has been training for the last two years to be a firefighter, identifies as genderqueer, feminist.

"Sometimes I feel more identified as female, and other times I feel more identified as male, depending on my situation. But then I start to think, It's based on the situations I'm in only because I'm thinking in terms of the definitions I've been taught. I feel like there's a struggle to cross borders and to keep things out. Confronting this will be important for feminism, but more generally for just figuring out how to coexist in the world."

SADYE, *TWENTY-THREE, COOPER SQUARE*

Native New Yorker, after-school teacher, artist, web designer, jeweler, feminist.

"I want to dedicate my life to utilizing art as a vehicle to educate, ignite, and mobilize youth. As a woman who works to create better opportunities for my students, I understand how necessary it is to be united and to build bridges amongst our sisters. We should all begin to acknowledge the power that love has in creating something better on behalf of something bigger."

SHARYN, *TWENTY-EIGHT, FORT GREENE*

Native of Sheepshead Bay, Brooklyn, bartender, graphic design student, from a traditional Moroccan-Israeli family, former punk, not sure if she's a feminist.

"Since I was a child, it has been banged into my head that I am to speak quietly and not have too many strong opinions. And I remember thinking, like, That's cool for you guys, but I'm American and I can do whatever I want. I was really young, but I was so angry about it!"

UNA, *TWENTY-FIVE, PARK SLOPE*

Raised in the East Village; teaches dance, political organizing, theater, poetry; performs her one-woman show at colleges and small theaters; relates to feminism but is wary of the academic version.

"A lot of the academic language about feminism makes me want to throw up. It doesn't feel accessible to the people who it matters to. Why does a person write it like that if most of us can't understand it? Of course, I know there's lots of great feminist theory. But it's just more meaningful to me to see women who don't necessarily need to articulate how they're feminists, they just exhibit it with everything they do."

SARA KANA, *TWENTY-NINE, SUNSET PARK*

Sara Kana, a.k.a. Lyric, born and raised in the Bronx, longtime hip-hop MC and rarely defeated freestyle battler, hosts hip-hop showcases, feminist.

"There are a lot of MCs who won't do songs with female rappers. At my first battle, all the men looked at me and instantly they judged. I was the only female there—you can't find a female to battle these days! If you lose and you're a woman, you feel that defeat like a brick in your chest because everyone's already expecting you to screw up."

BRAINSTORMERS, *LONG ISLAND CITY*

An art collective and performance group formed in 2005 that forces discussion about the insane gender disparities in the New York art world. Definitely feminists!

"People get angry when we point out the dearth of women in gallery shows. They'll say, 'The curators just pick the art based on what art is good!' But come on. If that's true, how come there are so many women accepted to MFA programs? Once they get to the commercial world, the number of women drastically drops. Does their work all of a sudden suck?"

JEANIE, *TWENTY-THREE, HARLEM*

Raised uptown in Manhattan, actress, former champion fencer, temp at a banking software company, feminist.

"My sister and I were always fighting this idea of what it was to be a 'girl.' We were very physical tomboys. I remember one summer, we went to this day camp upstate, and I was the only girl playing hockey with the boys. I wasn't afraid of being sweaty or being loud. We have always had that sense of 'We're different, and we're proud of that.'"

Likwuid

We meet Likwuid at a random Starbucks in Harlem between appointments. Likwuid, twenty-six, was born and raised in Columbia, South Carolina. She is a hip-hop artist and a personal trainer, and she is learning how to DJ. She offhandedly mentions that she also has her own company, Royalty Media Group, which works on changing how women are viewed in hip-hop. "I'm doing everything from online promotion, calling sponsors, following up with people. Owning your own business, you're never off the clock," Likwuid sighs.

Unprompted, Likwuid takes a shot at the feminist question. Like many, she's wary of the connotations, but makes a firm decision then and there that feminism applies to her life. To her, it just describes a strong woman who can stand on her own two feet. The word seldom comes up

> **"They're taking women out of the picture and saying hip-hop is dead! How you gonna have life with only one gender?"** —Likwuid

in Likwuid's daily life, though. She has never been asked the question. But she gets worked up when we raise the question of women and hip-hop. "There are numerous women that are making great music. But if you let the industry tell it, they say, 'Oh, women don't sell, women artists are too hard to work with, you gotta do their fashion, their budgets.' I'm like, 'Please, you got men walking around with blue chinchilla coats.' The excuses that come up with women, they just don't add up. The problem really is that hip-hop is so focused on objectifying women that they can't even step out and take an objective look at the situation."

Emma and I want to know the real reason that women artists don't sell. What's changed from the Salt-N-Pepa days? "These women aren't selling because they're creating the same Barbie over and over again. When we had Queen Latifah, MC Lyte, it was balanced, it was beautiful, they had their individual style. Now they're taking women out of the picture and people are saying hip-hop is dead. Of course it's dead! How you gonna have life with only one gender?"

LIKWUID

Laura

Laura Kipnis is the anti–Erica Jong, freely admitting that she has no interest in being a role model and doesn't have any particular advice for us. "I don't want to occupy myself with giving advice on how people's lives or political agendas should be." Still, she lets us pick her brain pretty thoroughly over several cups of coffee. Laura is a cultural and media critic who is also a professor at Northwestern University, but she's in New York a lot. She is originally from Chicago, which might explain why she appears to be so sick of it.

Laura has a strange relationship with feminism. "I wouldn't refuse the label," she says, "but to me, pinning yourself down to a particular identity doesn't feel useful. Sometimes I feel like a woman, and sometimes I don't." She tries to avoid being typecast as "the prosex feminist," telling us instead about her new book on scandal and a piece she's writing for *Playboy* about why conservative men hate Hillary. Laura has a hard time saying that feminism and women's issues are moving in a positive direction. "There's progress on one level, but there's so much competition and hatred between women."

Despite her suspicions of feminism, Laura hits us with tons of issues she thinks about. She explains her concern about women's obsession with how they look, what she calls the "hidden double shift." According to Laura, women are aware of this impediment, but simply feel defeated by it. "You can have read every feminist book on your bookshelf and still have issues about food and eating and the way your hair is styled," she points out.

It almost feels like Laura wishes her unpredictability could bleed into her feminine routines. But she seems all too aware of the connection between beauty and success in our looks-obsessed culture. "It helps you blend in and offers you more romantic and sexual opportunity—because that's still the way the heterosexual world is organized, despite all the supposed female progress."

LAURA

Jennifer

Jennifer Bartlett first caught Emma's attention when Emma read an entry on Jennifer's blog. It was the day after Jennifer had attended the panel, "Beyond the Waves, Feminist Artists Talk Across Generations," at the Sackler Center for Feminist Art, at the Brooklyn Museum, where Emma and her mother had spoken. Jennifer described a cornucopia of racial, sexual, and class sensitivity, but "as usual, disability was the glaring absence." She wrote about disabled women being so off the feminist radar that even the most PC thinkers gloss over them. Emma and I thought she was right, and we arranged to meet Jennifer at her apartment in Greenpoint to get her take on feminism.

Jennifer herself has cerebral palsy, which doesn't affect her mentally, but it does impact her motor skills and speech. She is unflinching and matter-of-fact—kind, but unapologetic. She is in her thirties, a poet and professor at Montclair State University, married with a son. She tells us that she is "grateful for feminism" but consciously rejects the term. Jennifer grew up in a matriarchal family where she took for granted that women can do what they want. "My family never gave me the message that I couldn't be powerful because I was a woman or because I was disabled."

"So then why doesn't feminism resonate?" we wonder aloud. To us, that exact sentiment is the principle of feminist activism.

"The way I have difficulty with society as a person with a disability so far overrides my difficulty as a woman," Jennifer explains. Plus, "I find feminism very contradictory. A lot of feminists make a point to list all of the minorities they cover, but they completely overlook disabled people." She believes that this exclusion stems from the fact that disabled women's issues are often quite different from mainstream feminism's agenda. Jennifer points out, for example, that "while feminism fights for equal pay, women with disabilities cope with being excluded from the job market entirely."

She echoes Carey Perloff, back in California, the theater director who pointed out that working-class women have double shifts and kids and bills to think about, and thus rarely have time to be feminist activists. But Jennifer promises us that being disabled isn't solely about being distracted by other struggles. It's also "being in an alien space" in terms of sexual objectification. "On a day-to-day basis I'm not objectified as a woman. People don't catcall handicapped people."

Jennifer adds last-minute that she does think she leads a feminist lifestyle. It just seems to be the PC aspect she objects to. "My hope is that one day full inclusion of minorities will happen organically. Now it seems kind of forced."

JENNIFER

Anne

Anne Waldman doesn't seem to quite know why we are in her Chelsea apartment, but she starts weaving us an intricate tale of her childhood and the post-Beat days in the East Village anyway. Anne has been a poet and performer in New York for decades. She tells us about her free spirit mother, "a cultural feminist" by way of her bohemian lifestyle. As for herself, Anne never associated with more radical feminists like Andrea Dworkin, and she instead calls herself a feminist because she "attended things"—readings, protests. It went with the downtown territory.

Above all, she tells us, her allegiance has always been to the "creative imagination." And when male dominance stood in the way of creativity, Anne was on board to fight it. For eight years, Anne ran the St. Mark's Poetry Project with the likes of Allen Ginsberg, Alice Notley, and Bernadette Mayer. "I always tried to bring women more into the mix."

Emma tells Anne of the few days on our road trip when we listened to Jack Kerouac's *On the Road*, and how we felt resentful of women's exclusion from those endless drunken philosophical discussions of the Beat Era. Anne rolls her eyes. "Oh, yes. It was totally apparent that women weren't let in on the secrets. Maybe it was my mother's example, but I always had the chutzpah to join in those late-night conversations."

WRITERS AND ARTISTS

The cramped, bustling intellectual hothouse of New York City is a well-known feminist refuge. Our journey focused on young women, but we couldn't resist going a little crazy and squeezing out some words of wisdom from our favorite writers and artists, some of whom we've known since childhood.

AMY

"Right now my cohort of feminist friends are talking about the hideousness of ageism, and the way it overlaps with gender. Among other injustices, men are still considered attractive after a certain age while women become invisible. There's a myth that older women are asexual, but really many of them are wondering, 'How are we going to get sex partners if men only want younger women?'"

—**Alix Kates Shulman**
best-selling Second Wave feminist writer, author of
Memoirs of an Ex–Prom Queen,
early and influential radical feminist activist

"My students say, 'Now we get to be individuals. We're not just women—we get to be people. Second Wave feminists used to say that there were no personal solutions, and young women are saying, 'On the contrary! We all get to have a personal solution!' Sometimes that delights me, that we made that possible. The only question is, can these individuals align together to do anything?"

—**Ann Snitow**
early and influential radical feminist
intellectual, writer, editor, and professor

"In the beginning, people gave Third Wave feminists an allowance, not an investment, like, 'You're so cute, I love what you're doing.' But at the same time we felt embraced and mentored by Gloria Steinem and others. We wanted to be appreciative."

—**Amy Richards**
Third Wave feminist writer and advice columnist,
cofounder of the Third Wave Foundation

ANN

COURTNEY

"Of course I believe that incredible outreach can be achieved with blogs, but there's a real value in visceral experience and the need to create dialogues like this, where we're sitting at a table and I can see you and get your essence. We haven't yet figured out a way to bring online ideas into something very real and physical."

—**Courtney Martin**
feminist journalist and blogger, author of Perfect Girls, Starving Daughters

"I feel nothing but excitement about the new generation of women. People look at things like Girls Gone Wild, or the fact that girls cut themselves, or violent body image issues, and think it's much worse now. But it's not true, it's not worse. Take the issue of early sexual contact, for instance: Certainly there are girls who aren't self-protecting, but there are also more girls in charge of their libidos and having a sense of sexual expression, before they find themselves being forty and finally getting their first vibrator."

—**Jennifer Baumgardner**
author, activist, filmmaker, Third Wave feminist, cofounder of the Third Wave Foundation

LINDA

"When women stop dropping out to take care of their babies, men won't be able to work at Goldman Sachs anymore. Then they'll be faced with the same problem as women: Do you want a fulfilling career or do you want a baby? But if these eighty-hour-a-week jobs didn't exist period, gender equity might be possible."

—**Linda Hirshman**
Second Wave feminist lawyer, journalist, and author

"The tension between different generations of feminists is less about age—that's more manufactured by the media. There's a bigger tension between grassroots and national organizations, which is divided not only by age but by class and race. I think online stuff can definitely help bridge the gap."

—**Jessica Valenti**
feminist, founder and executive editor of the blog Feministing, activist, author of Full Frontal Feminism *and* The Purity Myth

"In retrospect, people say that there was a separate feminist art movement, but I didn't really experience that. Women artists wanted more representation in galleries, in collections, and in museums, parity which we still don't have. You either made it in the man's world or you didn't make it—and most women didn't. I saw the women's artist movement as being important more because we were creating our own space."

—**Carolee Schneemann**
well-known visual and performance artist, often classified as a feminist artist because she works with her body and sexuality

"Being labeled a feminist artist can mean different things. There's gotta be an analysis of power from a gendered perspective. If you don't have that, that's very dangerous. But that doesn't mean you have to make art about your personal life or do paintings about your body!"

—**Mira Schor**
painter, author of Wet: On Painting, Feminism, and Art Culture *and coeditor with Susan Bee of* M/E/A/N/I/N/G

"I think your generation of female artists has to move on. For sure the feminist art community in New York needs new blood but you have to figure it out differently. Your art has to involve a greater population. I've always felt that I'm more interested in a much more inclusive population of women, not just women artists."

—**Joan Snyder**
New York, painter, and feminist who feels ambivalent about being labeled

JOAN

CAUGHT IN THE WEB

We had made a plan on the drive into New York that Emma's post-Christmas time would be better spent in her Chicago apartment logging some serious hours with the photos and our blog. Her departure inevitably leaves me to contemplate the larger impact of *Girldrive*'s site and other blogs as I prepare for my time in the city sans Emma. The online feminist community tapped into the *Girldrive* mission almost immediately. Invitations ensued. "Y'all should come to Mobile, Alabama. We have a pretty diverse group of feminists here!" Jamie of Feminists for Progress posted on our schedule. "If you find yourself near Columbus, Ohio, feel free to stop by my place!" posted another woman named Jen. We were touched by our devoted readers, but we didn't realize the full impact of online communities until we had a chance to sit down with some of the movers and shakers in the feminist blogosphere.

JESSICA

Before Emma leaves, we interview Jessica Valenti, the cofounder and executive editor of the highly trafficked feminist blog Feministing, who tells us that blogs make it possible for a young woman "to choose the level of her involvement. There is a stereotype that in order to be a feminist you have to be this big loud activist, but it is just as important if that girl from Fresno absorbs the ideas and has the networks at her fingertips."

SORAYA

Virtual feminism also ensures a diversity of voices that would be impossible to capture in local communities. Take Soraya, twenty-four, an online strategist for *The New York Times*, who insists that the blogosphere keeps big-city feminists on their toes. "In New York City," she explains, "you can have a dinner party and invite ten like-minded female friends and have a discussion about issues that pertain to you. Or, you can write something online and get reactions from women in Australia, Bali, Afghanistan. They're challenging you and posing new ideas, pushing you to be a different kind of feminist."

We still know that *Girldrive*'s blog could never be a substitute for the kind of indispensable bonds we've forged on our trip. All along we've been shying away from email interviews when face-to-face chats were not possible, knowing that there was nothing like following the ebbs and flows of a true peer-to-peer chill session.

LYN

Perhaps because of its impersonal nature, the Internet doesn't seem ideal for sparking an intergenerational conversation. For some older women, like feminist poet Lyn Hejinian, who we met in Berkeley, the social networking explosion is a perplexing trend. Lyn sees it as "dangerous to rely on these sites," as they can lead to false senses of community and obsession with faking a caricatured self-image.

Emma and I don't agree, but we can see where the Internet is largely the new language of youth. Some media-savvy older feminists see the value in being an online presence, like Susie Bright and Gloria Feldt, in their fifties and sixties, respectively. But others simply don't communicate that way.

JENNIFER

Even Jennifer Baumgardner, thirty-seven, admits to us that she feels "too old to be really good at being an online presence." Our best hope is that the exchange of information on the Internet will continue to ignite discussion in the real world as well, so that there's fluidity between different methods. After all these years, real discussion is still the most effective path to consciousness.

—Nona

Jessica

I gear myself up for the next stretch of interviews without Emma, who's well on her way to Chicago. As soon as I knock on the door of Jessica's Bay Ridge apartment, I immediately hear the excited whoops of her four-year-old daughter, Olivia—a nice greeting on this cold, drizzly day. Jessica, twenty-three, is native to Park Slope and just moved to this apartment a couple years ago. Her parents are both writers—her dad once wrote about her parents' marriage in a memoir ("pretty gruesome," she warns me). Her mom used to write for magazines but was diagnosed with Parkinson's disease when she was pregnant with Jessica and can't work too much anymore. Jessica married at eighteen and had Olivia soon after. Now she stays home to take care of Olivia and her marriage is on the brink of ending. She never went to college, so that's her main goal as soon as Olivia starts kindergarten—to study interior design or illustration.

"I definitely consider myself a feminist," she tells me. "Unconsciously, I did go the more old-fashioned route. People ask me all the time, 'What do you do?' And I've always felt a little reluctant to say, 'I stay home with my daughter.' Even when people say, 'You're such a great mom,' it just doesn't seem like enough for me." Jessica's husband is a pastry chef and works so much that she is unable to work herself. This work-home separation of parental roles, she says, "has been a really big issue. He has a career and I don't. I have this thing hanging over my head, that I don't have a college degree."

Although Jessica definitely admits, "things are hard," she resents that anyone would judge her feminism on her life choices. She doesn't think her life path is "unfeminist. I never had in my mind that *every* woman should get married young and have babies. That's just what I ended up doing."

In fact, Jessica believes that her feminism is very influenced by the fact that she has a daughter. "I'm really aware of the media and how it degrades women. It starts from a really young age. Like those Bratz dolls—Olivia doesn't have any of those, thank god—but they look like strippers!" Jessica laughs. "Part of me wishes that mothers would get involved in an anti-Bratz campaign or something." Beyond the media, Jessica notices, "Just walking down the street people are judging women everywhere. I don't ever want my daughter scrutinizing herself or comparing herself to the way women are 'supposed' to look."

Mehiko

Mehiko, twenty-three, is an old friend of mine who is, in her own quiet way, one of the most independent, iconoclastic women I've ever known. She wouldn't describe herself as an activist, but

JESSICA

would also never dream of subscribing to common wisdom simply because it was easier. She does her own thing and doesn't care if it sounds weird. Mehiko is the only child of Japanese immigrants—a seamstress mom and musician dad—and has lived in Williamsburg her whole life.

Mehiko is a feminist—not because "I do anything on a daily basis," but because "I am a product of feminism," which she feels automatically gives her license to be ironic about sexism. "Think about being raunchy or going to strip clubs or women making degrading jokes about other women—we can't do that without feminism. It's like counter-counter-culture. We can joke about these things and make light of them because there's nothing that's going to infringe our freedom because we're women." That startles me: Can women really do *anything* they want? "I guess not," Mehiko concedes, "but I don't feel many obstacles in my life."

I'm skeptical that nothing relating to being a woman pisses Mehiko off. She's one of the most headstrong women I know—hasn't she had one of those "This is bullshit" moments?

Mehiko's gender analysis develops when the topic of her recent singlehood comes up. A few months ago, she broke up with her boyfriend of three years, who had been expecting to move in with Mehiko and start a life together. Mehiko, fearful of never feeling completely independent,

broke it off and decided to sexually explore a bit. "I fucking hate that women have to be the ones to urge guys to put condoms on. I also hate the fact that it's seen as slutty to carry around condoms! I'd like to see girls not feel guilty about being sexually active and promiscuous. Girls are not there yet if I'm feeling weird about having condoms in my bag." Mehiko tells me of times when she's discussing her sexual escapades with her guy friends and they'll say, "You can't do that. Girls are sluts and guys are players and that's the way it is." Mehiko grimaces. "*That*," she says, pointing her finger, "is bullshit."

Pia M.

Pia and I meet at a café in Greenwich Village. It is loud and Pia speaks softly, but this girl has resolve. She is a busy, busy lady, juggling dancing, choreographing, managing a dance studio, and being an after-school teacher. She is twenty-five, was raised in Crown Heights, and now lives in Park Slope.

After a bit of thought, Pia decides she is not a feminist. It's not that she believes in societal gender roles, like men should wear pants and women wear skirts. But she does believe that there are some roles defined by nature, like men planting the seed and women carrying it. "I think a lot of gender roles are there for a reason," she says.

MEHIKO

Pia adds that feminism is definitely an academic term for her, and she's never heard her mom or any of her role models use the word. When Pia has come across feminism, it's always been in terms of African American studies and the marginalization of women of color in the movement. Pia makes it very clear that racial activism is a higher priority for her.

"The first step to getting racial equality in an American patriarchal society is getting some perks for your men, and then hoping that your men are going to turn around and try to get some perks for you. I feel like that's why a lot of black women don't label themselves as feminists. They'll label themselves as racial activists and then bring in women's issues as a second-tier thing. We are grappling with a whole different set of issues that just come first. I'm always reminded that I'm black before being reminded that I'm a woman."

Pia hasn't personally come across much sexism, even while working as a dancer. She does see that men are hesitant to be dancers because, she says, "Guys think, *Oh, it's not okay for me to dance—it must*

PIA

mean that I'm gay. It's a little bit ironic because the professional dance world is run by men—especially in European dance—but mostly gay men." Hmmm. I begin to pick up on some gender awareness. But Pia insists again that these inequalities are not at the top of her list. "It's not like I don't notice these things," she says, "but my attention is elsewhere."

Katha and Sophie

Katha Pollitt meets me in a typical Upper West Side diner. Katha is a writer who pens the Subject to Debate column in *The Nation*, and who, coincidentally, is working on a book called *Learning to Drive*. She is a no-holds-barred feminist—an admirer and admiree of my mom—and she has tons to say about our generation. "A lot of doors have been opened for women, and young women like you and my daughter have benefited from that," she says. But she worries that women our age think the struggle is over and think of feminism as a burden. "Calling yourself a feminist doesn't win you friends," she says. "It doesn't get you boyfriends."

Not that Katha doesn't have a deep respect for young feminists, citing Jessica Valenti and Ann Friedman as writers she reads all the time. Still, she thinks we have a lot of work to do in terms of framing our individual lives in a bigger context.

Katha singles out motherhood, for example, as

relatively uncharted territory for us. "Year after year," she explains, "new mothers find out, 'Oh great, I have to do all the housework, I have to cut back at work or even quit, why is it all on me?' But where is the movement for a national system of daycare? Nowhere." Katha acknowledges that mothers are in a less-than-ideal position to be activists—rich or poor, all moms scramble just to fit everything into their day. But Katha insists that women should have some prescience. "Women wait until it's too late to deal with these issues," she warns.

Katha didn't have her daughter until she was thirty-seven because she was always afraid that having a child would mean the end of an interesting life. Clearly this turned out not to be true, but, she tells us, "I had to scramble to keep my writing alive." As for her feminism, she says, "I always tried to pass feminist ideas on to my daughter. As to whether I was successful—well, you'll have to ask her about it."

A few days later, I have a chance to do just that. Sophie, Katha's effusive daughter, is an aspiring writer and has already published a book, along with three friends, called The Notebook Girls. Sophie, twenty, has a real problem with the word "feminist," but it's not because she doesn't have women's issues on her mind constantly. It's more like this: "If I lived outside the New York intellectual bubble, I think I would have to call myself a feminist, because I would be up against so much more. But to me, in my life, I resent there having to be a word. There's no word for pro-gay-rightsist or blacklist, so why should I have this word that puts me in this isolated world called feminism just because I believe in basic human rights?"

Being raised by feminist mamas isn't the only thing Sophie and I have in common. She and I—both straight and undeniably girly—played on Wesleyan's rugby team. The teams inhabit a strong lesbian community, a fact that forced both of us to think a lot about gender roles. "It's been really hard to be one of the only straight people on the team," Sophie tells me.

She feels strongly about a years-long debate surrounding the team's name. A few years ago the team was reanointed Wesrugby, rather than Women's Rugby, to be more inclusive. Sophie thinks this is ridiculous. "I wish it was called Women's Rugby. The reason I feel proud about being on the team is because we are women doing stuff that most people don't expect women to do. There's a certain bond that girls can make with each other so easily, and I love that."

SOPHIE AND KATHA

CHAPTER 11 — **Gusty Winds May Exist** →

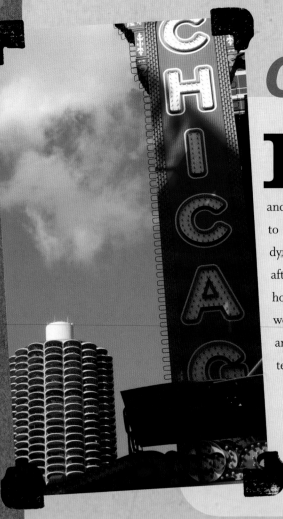

CHICAGO

For the second time in three months, I prepare to make the voyage from New York to Chicago alone—only this time I'm not coming back for a while. Emma has been living in Chicago since she graduated last spring, and she convinced me during our New York trip to move there. "If we're going to finish up *Girldrive* right," she coaxed me, "we need to settle in a city that's dynamic yet affordable—a city exactly like Chicago." So, a few days after New Year's, I brave the icy roads to meet Emma in our new home base. Our winter goal is to comb Chicago for interesting women, then make our way up to Wisconsin. But it's January, and I'm a bit worried about the Midwest's formidable winter temper.

Amalia

If you live anywhere near the North Side of Chicago, you know about Kuma's Corner. It's a packed, cacophonous burger joint where the heavy metal drowns out conversation and burly men knock you over left and right. The testosterone practically spills out onto the sidewalk. But most people don't know one little fact—the executive chef of Kuma's is a twenty-four-year-old woman.

Amalia meets me at a dive bar across the street from her work after a grueling lunch shift. She grew up in Minneapolis in a liberal, interracial household where she spent most of her time "building things, doing art, and mixing spices in the kitchen cabinet." She moved to Chicago to go to art school but then realized that she didn't want to do art for money. That's when she enrolled in culinary school and shortly afterward got hired at Kuma's.

In the span of a year and a half, Amalia has gone from line cook to head chef. Although she notes the high turnover—"you have to have a thick skin to work here"—she doesn't chalk up her success to luck. "The first time I walked in, the owner told me two things: 'One, women don't work in my kitchen, and two, when they do, they never stay long.' All I thought was, 'Good, you just gave me a challenge!'"

Amalia busted her ass for nine months, taking no days off and refusing to buckle under the pressure when she got bitched out in Kuma's sweltering, high-stress kitchen. "The reason men give for not wanting female chefs is because they think women are too emotional," she tells me. "And I think it's true. I do feel like going and crying downstairs, but I don't. I take it to heart and never again make that mistake I got yelled at for."

Amalia has always felt that it's her "duty" to be a strong, assertive woman. So is she a feminist? "I don't think so," Amalia says. "Men are a great asset to my life, and I don't wish they didn't exist." Is that what she thinks feminism is—wishing men didn't exist? She shrugs. "That's how it's always been explained to me." She associates the word with the "feminist man-hating dyke" caricature, the kind of women who only need men to procreate. Being queer herself, she gets upset if people see her that way. "Most of my friends are guys!" she says.

Still, she gets riled up about a number of gender issues. She hates it when men holler at her on the street. She's pissed off that many guys think lesbians are just heartbroken straight women in disguise. She seethes when she hears over and over again from men that "the only kitchen a woman should be in is at home." But she credits them as making her a stronger person. "I'm grateful for that douche bag who hits on me because he gives me that much more adrenaline to prove him wrong. Everything I've accomplished is because somebody told me I couldn't."

AMALIA

Katharine

One frigid day downtown, we meet up with Katharine, a twenty-three-year-old resident of Forest Park, Illinois, who is studying to be a librarian and working at two nonprofits downtown. She also has another possible title in her future: nun. She has resolved to either fall in love with a man and devote herself to a family or become a nun and devote herself to God and those who need help. Katharine, at first glance, does not fit any chaste stereotypes, coming across as a perfectly normal, stylish, cool twentysomething. But she holds some very traditional ideals about gender, specifically about sex. Quite simply, "The male is the giver, and the woman is the receiver." She is openly pro-life and she believes a woman should wait to have sex until she is married. But Emma wants to know: "Is it ever okay for a woman to have sex just . . . because?"

Katharine's answer is no. She sees casual sex and the use of birth control as the same sin: not accepting the whole person—"their body, brain, and soul." Casual sex ignores a person's soul and reduces that person to an object. Contraception in a loving relationship still eliminates an aspect

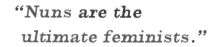

> "Nuns are the ultimate feminists."
> —Katharine

of a woman's whole being—her fertility. And even though Katharine gushes about the profound sisterhood of being a nun and having female friendships, she applies the same logic to homosexual relationships. "Sex, by its very nature, is life-giving," she says, and any sexual relationship that gets in the way of that is denying our purpose—it's "a counterfeit union."

As for feminism, Katharine has no problem with the word. She even calls a nun "the ultimate feminist" because she is rejecting many of the traps that the modern woman gets wrapped up in. Katharine explains, "Nuns are looking at the world and saying, 'Listen, you want to care about what your clothes look like? I don't care. You want to care about making money? I don't make any money! You want to cast down those who are burdened? I want to pick them up.' She has given up her entire life, her clothes, her cool shoes, just so that she can help people who don't have help. That's really empowering."

KATHARINE

Alex J.

Alex is one of Emma's friends from the University of Chicago who Emma has been excited to interview since the beginning of *Girldrive*. We catch her on her second-to-last day in the States before she leaves on a long backpacking trip through Morocco. Alex was born in the States and grew up in New England with her mom and her sister after living in Pakistan for a couple years. Her dad still lives there, and Alex herself just spent the last month in the country. After her forthcoming Morocco trip, she will move to Tunisia to do an intensive study of Arabic there for six months.

She says yes to being a feminist, but says it is hard to define what kind of feminism she identifies with. "Is it Western feminism, Islamic feminism, women-of-color feminism? I believe in legal and civil equality of women, but I also realize it's an alienating term to a lot of people." Unlike many of our other interviewees, Alex sees feminism's exclusivity on a global scale, calling the American version "Eurocentric." "Western feminism automatically sees Islam as a constraint to women," Alex explains. "It says, 'The veil or *hijab* is always a sign of evil patriarchy' or, 'Every single woman in an Islamic country is repressed and oppressed.' That lack of cultural understanding gets me really riled up."

After visiting Pakistan, Alex sees a lot of feminist potential in a Muslim state despite the dominance of men in the public sphere. She's even brought in a list of Islamic feminists for us to look over, a list that includes assassinated Pakistani Prime Minister Benazir Bhutto and author and professor Leila Ahmed. "Within these cultures, there's a push for female equality and women's liberation," Alex says. And she doesn't think the religion of Islam needs to be in conflict with feminism, either.

Another gender issue that Alex ponders has less to do with global feminism: She's noticed a kind of "dated urgency in young women in America to want to get married." She sees an increasing pattern of young women falling into traditional roles and putting their careers on the back burner. But Alex catches herself and asks, unprompted, "Why should I be critical of these roles? I don't think feminism needs to be defined by a career." Alex concludes that she just hopes for more dialogue about this in the future.

Her number one future priority, though, is to "make feminist discourse see cultural nuances. The world is becoming ever more globalized. People have to realize that things can't keep existing in a binary."

ALEX

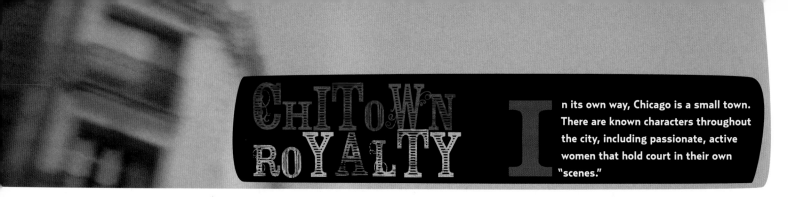

CHITOWN ROYALTY

In its own way, Chicago is a small town. There are known characters throughout the city, including passionate, active women that hold court in their own "scenes."

AMY SCHROEDER, *THIRTY-ONE, OLD TOWN/ LINCOLN PARK*

Founder and editor-in-chief of the women-focused pop culture magazine *Venus Zine*, through-and-through Midwesterner, Third Wave feminist.

"In our new issue of Venus, we have a feature on the Greatest Female Guitarists of All Time. I hate doing that in a way because it's ghettoizing women. Yet if we don't do this list, then chances are these women won't be recognized anywhere else. It sucks to be thought of as always the 'female guitarist,' but somebody's gotta recognize them."

AMY GALPIN, *THIRTY-TWO, WEST TOWN*

Gallery coordinator for Woman Made Gallery in Chicago, Midwest regional coordinator for the Feminist Art Project, adjunct art history professor at DePaul University, feminist.

"It seems there is a gap in terms of how younger artists are getting involved with feminism and making it relevant to their lives. There are young artists who don't want to show here. They don't want to make the distinction that their work is only supposed to be shown at a woman's gallery. They don't want the issue of personal identity associated with their work."

VERONICA ARREOLA, THIRTY-FOUR, WEST ROGERS PARK

Native Chicagolander, veteran feminist blogger, director of University of Illinois at Chicago's Women in Science and Engineering Program, feminist.

"Part of the challenge that the current generation has had with feminism is that the wall we used to hit, in science and in other fields, is getting further and further away. Women are now the majority of people going to college. The barriers come later in a career, and so does the feminist awakening."

ALEX WHITE, TWENTY-TWO, LOGAN SQUARE

Born and raised on the North Side of Chicago, front woman for the bands White Mystery and Miss Alex White & the Red Orchestra, DePaul University business graduate, operations manager at Busy Beaver Button Company.

"I just spoke at a panel discussion for the Chicago Music Commission, and I was there with a bunch of male record label owners. They were being so cynical, and I couldn't help but see a dark cloud over the audience's head. All of a sudden I felt this nurturing thing where I thought, These people can't leave uninspired. I don't know if I'm being stereotypical, but I felt like since I was the only woman I had to bring the more emotional side to it."

LAUREN BERLANT, FIFTY-TWO, HYDE PARK

Writer, professor of English at University of Chicago, influential feminist thinker.

"As an intellectual—feminist or not—you are constantly being called to say what you are thinking and describe what you are doing. Then there are these spaces for an interruption or a relief—the 'appetite' spaces, like eating and fucking. What feminism hoped for was forms of pleasure that would also be about self-development, where your forms of self-cultivation would also be your pleasure. But we have to admit that pleasure cannot just be about eloquence, culture, clarity. It's also about fogginess and sex. Once you think about sex as a place where you lose control, it's to some extent contrary to intellect and feminism as a theory. If feminism is about control, and sex is about losing control, how do you reconcile that?"

ALEX (TOP); LAUREN (BOTTOM)

Deliza

A couple months after I moved to Chicago, Emma and I started to help teach a photojournalism class at North Grand High School run by the non-profit Step Up Women's Network. Deliza is one of the girls in our class. She is sixteen and was raised in Puerto Rico and Chicago's Humboldt Park neighborhood. Deliza was initially drawn to a different Step Up class—one that focused on wellness. Deliza chose the class because, she tells us, "it was all girls, and it was about health. I mean, who can't benefit from a class like that?" Two years later, she has been deeply affected by it. "I learned to be healthier and accept my body. The class also changed the way I treated people, and definitely the way I treated girls. It helped me choose the right friends." She plays softball and plans to be a famous singer/dancer/choreographer. Before our interview starts, she brings us into her pantry–turned–music studio and serenades us with an R&B track she wrote herself.

An hour later over brunch, Deliza freely tells us her steadfast opinions on everything from teen pregnancy to women's roles in the Latino community, but she admits she has never heard of "feminism." Emma and I try as best we can to

DELIZA

explain the many facets of what feminism could mean. We give her a little history, and tell her that it's all wrapped up in choices, happiness, sex, family, and love. Remembering a particular day at the high school, we quote one of Deliza's fellow Step Up girls, Mary Ann, who told us that "being a feminist is not feeling like you just have to be barefoot in the kitchen and pop out babies."

Deliza ponders all of this and decides that feminism sounds good to her. "I believe I could do whatever I want, and no one's going to stop me. Not a man, not a female, not the government—I am my own person. So with the definition that you guys have given me, I would see myself as a feminist."

Out of nowhere, Deliza suddenly confesses to us that she was sexually assaulted when she was nine. "I'm fine now," she tells us. Her voice wavers. She tells us that her peace with the incident has to do with her religion: "I really struggled with forgiveness, but now that I've started to go to church, I've forgiven the man who hurt me. It was wrong, it was a mistake he did, but in God's eyes I'm still a virgin. I'm still pure."

Deliza tells us that she wants to incorporate her story into her singing career. "I know I can be an inspiration to other girls who this has happened to—that it's not all about being hidden and being trapped in your own body. I want to let girls know that they can have a voice."

THE GATEKEEPER

My heart breaks after we hear Deliza's story, not only because she had been hurt, or because she was only a child when it happened, but because she clearly feels stained by what happened. No matter how she has let her life blossom, the most important thing to restore after she was sexually assaulted was her "purity"—her virginity. Her belief that she has gotten a second chance at guarding her sexuality is associated with her faith. And she had told us in her interview that she barely lets her boyfriend touch her. On some level I feel that she was admitting to us that she will forever think of sex as something to defend herself against, not to enjoy.

I leave the interview feeling a mix of relief and rage. I'm glad that Deliza has a supportive family, and that she is able to talk so freely with us. But still—will our country's obsession with virginity ever end? Rape will always be unthinkably painful, but I can't help thinking that it could be a lot easier to heal from without the added pressure girls have to be the "gatekeepers." —*Nona*

MILWAUKEE

Emma and I have planned our Wisconsin excursion on the worst possible weekend imaginable. The drive to Milwaukee is usually only an hour and a half, but it's taking forever because of the sideways hail attacking the cars from all directions. Once the traffic breaks up, we feel our tiny Chevy sway from side to side just as we lay our eyes on a sign reading GUSTY WINDS MAY EXIST. *Understatement of the century*, we think.

We eventually arrive in Milwaukee safe and sound, and we wake up the next morning to a beautiful day. Our first order of business: a tour around Milwaukee's Bay View neighborhood, the home of the city's feminist bookstore, Broad Vocabulary.

Jessica

As a result of poor planning, our only course of action in Milwaukee is to strike up a spontaneous conversation with an unsuspecting subject. Luckily, Jessica, who works behind the desk at Broad Vocabulary, is more than down. She is twenty-seven, was born in Milwaukee, was an education major at UW–La Crosse, and works at a small alternative high school for "at-risk" youth on the South Side.

Jessica started volunteering here in the summer when she was off from teaching. She notes that parts of Milwaukee haven't changed much in years. "Two guys or two girls walking down the street holding hands will still turn heads," she says. Jessica tells us that the owners of this bookstore wanted to open this place not as a money-making profit enterprise, but "to let people know that feminism isn't a scary thing, that it's not penis-hating women running around crazy."

She watches quite a few gender issues being played out among her students. "The mentality of a lot of teenage boys is that girls are bitches and hos. The girls seemingly put up with it." Jessica sees teaching as a chance to be a role model for young women who may not stand up for themselves. "I try to present myself as a woman who makes a fuss for what I believe in."

JESSICA

MADISON

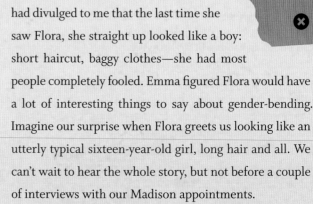

In Madison, we are staying with Emma's cousin, Susan David Bernstein, a professor of English at University of Wisconsin, who has a teenage daughter, Flora. Emma had divulged to me that the last time she saw Flora, she straight up looked like a boy: short haircut, baggy clothes—she had most people completely fooled. Emma figured Flora would have a lot of interesting things to say about gender-bending. Imagine our surprise when Flora greets us looking like an utterly typical sixteen-year-old girl, long hair and all. We can't wait to hear the whole story, but not before a couple of interviews with our Madison appointments.

Jackie

Jackie is a student of Susan's husband and agrees to meet us on short notice in her dorm. Jackie is twenty-two and from the suburbs of Chicago. She is a senior sociology major at UW-Madison, a lover of music, and a setter on the varsity volleyball team. Lately, the sport has been the focus of her life—she even plans on becoming a college coach when she graduates. Jackie says being an athlete gives her a healthy attitude about her body, but she admits that this is not true for everyone. "A lot of volleyball players have eating disorders," she says. "It's hard, because you're in little shorts and everyone is looking at you."

Jackie is not a feminist because "people think of 'feminist' as an extreme position, and I tend not to be extreme about anything." But that doesn't mean Jackie ignores issues about gender. She wants to "shatter some of the definitions of what it means to be a woman. You can be strong and

"You can be strong and still be feminine." —Jackie

still be feminine; you can be loud and active but still be sensitive."

Jackie sometimes gets annoyed at the rude reactions guys have to her muscular, six-foot build. "I'll be out and a guy will come up to me, and instead of starting a typical conversation like, 'How are you, what's your name?' it's, 'Whoa, you could beat me up!'" Jackie finds that male athletes are easier to date because they come from the same world. But any time she's ventured out of the circle, she's disappointed because a guy will often see her as "just an athlete. It's part of who I am, but not all of who I am—and sometimes guys don't see that."

Katie

Katie meets us at Susan's house with her small daughter in tow. She is twenty-six, grew up in Wausau, Wisconsin, and is a single mom to eight-year-old Kaitlin. She works two jobs—at a domestic abuse agency and a captioning company—and graduated from UW-Madison in 2006. This week marks her first week

JACKIE

KATIE AND HER DAUGHTER KAITLIN

of freedom from grad school applications, which she slaved over for months.

We don't hide our surprise about Katie's academic success—she's had a daughter to think about since she was eighteen! Katie acknowledges that she's had "a little more luck and opportunity" than most other mothers in her position. "My grandfather set aside some money for me and my brother and sister to pursue school," she explains. But this doesn't mean that she's blind to the realities of other single moms. "My friend has a daughter who's Kaitlin's age, and she can only take one or two classes because she has to work during the day and night. And she's going for nursing, which isn't something she is all that interested in. It was a very practical decision. Once she gets a degree she'll be able to support her daughter in the way that she wants to." We think back to our conversation with the mom in Sioux Falls who cursed her liberal arts degree and its uselessness. I'm beginning to feel more thankful than ever that I was able to pursue my own interests and not have to think about whether what I wanted to do was going to support my family.

> **"I never want to be one of those scholars who doesn't venture off campus."** —Katie

Katie adamantly identifies with feminism and feels passionately about reproductive healthcare. She argues politics with her parents all the time. "They think I'm brainwashed from the university," she laughs. She relates this disconnect to Wisconsin in general—there is a huge culture clash between Madison and the rest of the state. Madison, a city largely composed of professors and students, is a "liberal pocket" amid "guns, pickup trucks, and racism." Katie's goal is to be a professor herself, but she's promised herself not to "live in the ivory tower. I want to relate all this theory to real-life issues; the women I work with at the domestic violence shelter don't have time to protest. I never want to be one of those scholars who doesn't venture off campus."

Flora

Flora is sixteen, soft-spoken, and serious, barely cracking a smile during our conversation. She tells us that since Madison is "pretty liberal," she doesn't feel very limited by her gender at all. She doesn't relate to feminism because she's "not active in those things." Although she's sure there's probably some subtle sexism in her city, the issues most on her mind are doing well on the varsity track team and getting into college.

Despite being so fresh from her stylistic transformation, Flora understands exactly why she decided to change her appearance so drastically from tomboyish to feminine right before high school. "It made things easier. I had to put up with a lot of harassment—inconveniences like getting weird looks in the women's bathroom," she says. According to Flora, there's no one in her high school who seems to experiment with or cross gender lines.

At first, Flora says she has no idea where the impulse to dress like a boy came from. But a few minutes later, she amends her statement. "It's

just a better deal for boys. Women get the shorter end of the stick. The way people are treating Hillary Clinton, for instance; it just seems that a lot of people are okay with sexism." Even so, Flora doesn't see herself going back to her masculine look. "It's just harder to not be normal—and not only in high school." Flora is skeptical about gender norms changing any time soon. "Stereotypes are deeply incorporated in our society," she says. "It's really, really far down the road when those lines will be broken down more."

This is all Flora will tell us before she suits up to take a run—even though there's six inches of snow outside. "Damn," Emma says under her breath. "That's dedication!" She follows Flora outside and snaps a photo, just as the snow begins to blanket the back yard.

> ## "It's just harder not to be normal."
>
> **—Flora**

FLORA

CHAPTER 12 - - **Summers Past** - →

PHILADELPHIA

Come June, our bank accounts and schedules allow us to finally plan the last stretch of *Girldrive*—the East Coast. By the time we got back to New York last November, the weather was frigid and the snow was piling up. A devil-may-care road trip just wouldn't have felt the same. But as soon as the summer warmth rolls around, we know we have to get back on the road. We bite the bullet and drive twelve hours straight to the southern-most part of our eastern seaboard stretch, Philadelphia.

Thembi and Cille

Cille has been trying to get us to come to Philly for months. She's a friend of my best friend who got our initial mass email and has been down with *Girldrive* since its inception. Cille is twenty-four, a proud Philly native, and currently working for the city in emergency management. She is trying to pursue a master's in public policy and a law degree to become "Condoleezza Rice, if she weren't working for the Republicans."

She recruits one of her friends, Thembi, to come over and share a bottle of wine and good conversation. Thembi, twenty-nine, went to Harvard, is originally from Philly, and works for an educational testing service. But she really wants to be a "media maven—a writer and a talking head." She writes a blog called What Would Thembi Do? which she describes as a "black pop culture, random ridiculousness, Generation X, nostalgia-driven blog," among other things. Thembi is a feminist. "I think everyone's supposed to be one," she says. She believes in basic rights for women, even though she's pretty sure "biology drives a lot of social constructs around gender."

Cille isn't so sure. She relates to the term "womanist" more than "feminist," explaining that it has a "spiritual essence" in it that you can't separate from the black female experience. Cille thinks "feminist" feels too political and not connected enough to the spirit. "Womanist thinking

is always based in theology," she explains. "In particular, it relates to black women and how we've been able to use the spirit of the Creator to heal our families and ourselves, and to take care of people and be the breadbaskets and mules of the world. What has sustained us over that time has been a spirit, whether it be God, or whatever you believe in."

We talk for hours at Cille's house—about being a woman in the workplace, gay guys dominating women's industries and women's health, among other issues. Finally, the wine is gone and the bustle of the party next door is beckoning us. Cille warns us that it might be a weird scene, but the neighbors call out to us on the balcony and welcome us to join the fun.

We arrive and are instantly offered Jell-O shots from a guy wearing a shirt that reads SWALLOW OR IT'S GOING IN YOUR EYE. *He can't be serious*, I think. "Where'd you get that shirt?" we ask. "What's the deal?" He shrugs and says he got it on vacation with his brother. "But why is that funny? Are you trying to pick up girls? I don't *get* it," Emma presses on. The dude laughs nervously. We eventually drop it, assuming that he's probably a nice enough guy who doesn't realize the implications of a T-shirt like that. When we make our way into the next room, with a keg and a bunch of scantily clad women, we are reminded yet again how much work there is to do.

THEMBI (TOP); CILLE (BOTTOM)

Nathan

Nathan, like Cille, had been in touch with us from the beginning. "I'll tell you now—I'm not a woman," warned Nathan in his email. "I'm a transgendered man, but I love talking about feminism with my friends, on the Internet, and even to my own mother." It felt important to us to tap into the transgendered community, so on our second day in Philly, we're excited about the prospect of getting Nathan's perspective.

Nathan is twenty-two and grew up in Philly. He went to Bryn Mawr up until last year, when he quit college. He now works for a pharmaceutical software company, and although he hasn't gotten top surgery, he takes testosterone and fully passes as a man. He has always related to feminism, and when he was living life as a lesbian, he dated strictly self-proclaimed feminists. He doesn't think his transition affects that stance because, he tells us, "The reason I transitioned is unrelated. My understanding of feminism is for both sexes to be equal—in ability, capacity, rights, everything. I can't say that switching really takes away from that."

In fact, now that Nathan considers himself a man, he feels he can make a feminist difference "from the inside" when he's privy to misogynist conversations. "I don't pull out the whiteboard and write, 'Here's how not to objectify your wife,'" he jokes, "but I do express feminist ideals covertly, and I think it helps when guys hear it coming from guys."

Nathan thinks he's definitely more sensitive to sexist comments than a biological man would be—"there's a level of ignorance sometimes that you would think is just made up"—but at the same time, he's noticing some very real differences in his attitude now that he's been taking testosterone for so long. "Before I was taking T, I was empathetic, good at dealing with relationship problems, I could get into my girlfriend's head during arguments. A year later, that's all changed. Sometimes I'm like, 'Why are you crying?'" Does he understand male privilege now that the whole world thinks he's male? "Yes!" Nathan says emphatically. "People pay more attention to me. I don't feel like I have to prove my knowledge anymore."

Nathan doesn't see that as an excuse for men to use, though. "I believe that hormones can all be surmounted by sheer application of will." He also assures us that testosterone hasn't affected his ability to see women as equals. He just thinks men have to work a little harder, and feminists have to force them. "Feminism is wonderful, but nobody notified the guys to get behind this, to accept the fact that they need to give up a little privilege."

NATHAN

PRÓVIDENCE

The next morning, we head up to Providence to cold-visit a young feminist's art collective called Dirt Palace—a kooky artist's absolute heaven, if their website is any indication. We have been trying to contact these women for weeks but didn't realize until today that one of Emma's good friends, Brian, dated one of the artists! Here we see our "in." Within minutes we not only have an invitation to visit the Palace from artists named Pippi and Xander but also a place to crash for the night.

DIRT PALACE

The Dirt Palace is beyond our wildest artistic dreams. The place is a seemingly never-ending treasure chest of dolls, stickers, posters, books, mirrors, musical instruments, yarn, fabric, records, movies, and hundreds more—each room capturing its own whimsical theme.

Originally an abandoned library building, the collective has a library of its own—S.S.C.O.W.L. (Shivering Shelves Collection of Weirdness Library).

Even the kitchen is wonderfully intricate, displaying an eight-foot-high grid of hundreds of square food photos and a refrigerator adorned with countless revolutionary bumper stickers and magnets.

Emma's camera can hardly keep up with the nooks of creativity before her eyes. Between photo snaps, she gushes, "I wanna live here when I grow up!"

—Nona

Xander

After wandering around the library–turned–artist abode for what seems like hours, we finally settle down in the kitchen to pick the brain of Xander, one of the original members of Dirt Palace. She's thirty-three, was born in DC, and grew up on Long Island. "I think the suburbs are usually pretty terrible, but they make you creative in a lot of ways," she muses. She works at a nonprofit art space as a managing director and has lived in Providence for fifteen years. And of course, she is an artist, which is why she cofounded Dirt Palace in 2000. The idea was originally a not-for-profit, but then some of the women decided they wanted a "home base." Xander and another resident, Pippi, bought this building shortly thereafter and redesigned it from the ground up.

Xander tells us that "of course" she is a feminist, that she doesn't really understand the reluctance to identify with it. "Except," she amends, "maybe that there was a certain kind of anger that came with the first waves of feminism, and I can understand not wanting to own that anger—it can be consuming!" She tells us that earlier in her life, her art was "part of a women's tradition," experimenting with fabrics and quilts, conscious of this rich history that's been kept out of fine art. Later, though, she started printmaking and producing films—doing animation, using puppets, and sometimes with "real humans."

Xander thinks a lot about "global capital" and the "economy of the world," which she sees as feminist issues. "I like the fact that I have a political life that's separate from my art," she says. For Xander, her "utopic sci-fi" hope for the future is that "as long as no one is being pushed to ultra-femme or subservient because the marketplace wants that, if all those things could come from a place of equality, then that could be a really interesting and exciting understanding of gender."

XANDER

BÓSTON

We had originally planned to sidestep Boston in order to pay a visit to our old summer camp in western Massachusetts. But when two other young artists living in the city contact us, we decide to continue our tour of the East Coast artist scene and stay in Boston for a night. We end up staying with my mom's ex-boyfriend, Steve, a gentle soul who had a Jesus beard and dropped acid on a regular basis back in 1969. Steve met my mother when she was on her own road trip to Colorado Springs to join the antiwar GI coffeehouse movement. Over dinner that night, he recounts those early days with her, telling us that even back then my mother was an ardent feminist. Steve's voice is even-keeled and quiet, but we can tell he's proud that we're following in my mom's footsteps.

Jeanne and Rachelle

Jeanne and Rachelle heard about *Girldrive* from Maria Elena Buszek and Joanna Frueh, who they met at a conference. A short while later they excitedly emailed us wanting to meet up. We bask in the hot Boston sun as we chat with the two women over ice cream cones.

Jeanne, twenty-seven, was raised in Reno and just graduated from the Rhode Island School of Design's MFA program. She's already been offered a job teaching one class at Brown University this fall, which was enough to keep her in the

JEANNE AND RACHELLE

Boston area. Jeanne is also a working artist who's going to have a solo show in Tulsa on "knitting as computing."

Rachelle, twenty-eight, is originally from New Hampshire. She went to Catholic college in Worcester, Massachusetts, and then went to RISD. She is now teaching at Chester College of New England in New Hampshire, after having taught at Keene State College last year.

Both women are feminists, but each came to identify with it differently. Jeanne's teenage years were spent in the hardcore music scene, "after dramatically exiting Christianity," she adds sardonically. She spent years wanting to start a band, "but the guys I knew in Reno didn't want to be in bands with girls. Finally, when I was twenty-two, I got asked to be a singer in a band with three boys. I was instantly a role model for women." After performing, she discovered a talent that incited admiration from local women. "There weren't any women screaming the way the men were screaming. Except me! The community really noticed that."

Rachelle tells us about her own feminist awakening, which she sees as similar to Jeanne's, though it played out in a different realm. Growing up in frosty New Hampshire, ice hockey was *the* thing for boys to do—and she wanted to do it, too. She ended up being the one girl on a team of boys. She also played on a RISD coed ice hockey

> # "I'm not against those organizations for feminist artists, but when are we going to stop needing them?"
>
> —Jeanne

team called the RISD Nads. Jeanne assures us that "Rachelle was awesome." She gives Rachelle a look before adding, "Although one time she got knocked down by a boy and it was really scary," explaining that there are definite downsides to playing on coed teams of very physical sports.

Emma is anxious to talk about art. "Tell us about some work you've been doing!" she implores eagerly. Jeanne whips out her computer and shows us a video she did in 2007: a slo-mo portrayal of her getting punched in the face by another woman. Rachelle tells us about a piece she displayed as a visiting professor, which was subsequently censored and resulted in her not getting hired back. The piece was called *Cheer! Shorts*, which was a play on cheerleader shorts that have cutesy, flirty expressions imprinted on the butt. Rachelle replaced the more innocuous

phrases with explicit versions, like UNUSUALLY WET PUSSY or COCK-SUCKING QUEEN. Some of the faculty were outraged, and "they put a curtain over my work so it couldn't be seen," she tells us. "But I thought it was a good thing. When you do something like that, it just makes it more enticing."

We ask the obvious question: Would they call these pieces "feminist art"? Rachelle says yes, that she is making a direct link to the C.U.N.T. cheerleaders, a 1970s feminist art performance group of students at California State University. Jeanne hesitates to label her work. "Eighty percent of my work has to do with being a woman, but it seems like you have to choose, like do you want to be an artist or a feminist artist? I don't think that's okay. I'm not against those organizations for feminist artists, but when are we going to stop needing them?"

TÓLLAND

Óur next stop is a pilgrimage to our old summer camp, Camp Kinderland, in Tolland, Massachusetts, the place where Emma and I first met. Neither of us have been back in six years, and the distance has been bittersweet. We loved camp—it was a place where social justice was front and center, and we formed a lot of our ideals there. But though there was a lot of discussion about the Civil Rights Movement, the war in El Salvador, and the Holocaust, we never once remembered having talked about feminism. A couple months earlier, we had written Kinderland's director, suggesting a workshop about gender issues, and he had agreed. We can't wait to see if a little feminist history has since been imbued in the camp's curriculum—and if it hasn't, we're prepared to change that.

—**Nona**

EMMA AND NONA AT CAMP, ALL DRESSED UP FOR BANQUET, IN 1998

CAMP

We spend an entire day hosting coed workshops, tailoring our one-hour sessions to different age groups. With the eleven-year-olds, we spark a conversation about gender stereotypes by going around in a circle asking, "What's the first thing that comes to your mind when someone says 'boy'? What about 'girl'?" We divide the older kids into pairs and lay out a bunch of magazines and ask them to deconstruct what a "positive" and "negative" image means to them.

We get mixed results. The thirteen-year-old girls are enraptured by the magazine discussion, and they pepper us with questions for fifteen minutes after they are dismissed. The boys are a little more grumbly. Later, we find out that they complained to their counselors that the workshops were "stupid." We laugh and shake our heads. We can only hope it makes sense someday!

The next day is spent roaming our old stomping grounds, soaking in the nostalgia that peeks through every corner. So many years have gone by since we spent summers here as insecure teens, stressing about cliques and bathing suits and makeout sessions in the Grape Arbor. We both agree: We could have used some feminist thinking back then to guide us through the muck.

NORTHAMPTON

Northampton is a half an hour from Camp Kinder-land, so we take a day to explore the famously left-leaning town. Emma and I are hit with a whole new host of memories—during our camp years, Northampton was the destination of a once-a-summer brush with civilization, an interruption from the shelter of Kinderland, a place where money, time, and real-world problems seemed distant. Now, years later, the city seems less like a field trip and more like yet another opportunity for some feminist discovery.

LANI, TWENTY-TWO, HAMPSHIRE STUDENT, FEMINIST, MEMBER OF TRANSLATE GENDER

"I remember having one of those moments where I was like, Oh my god, I'm a feminist! *That said, it's not an identity that I necessary use, because I don't think there's one feminism, and I think we get bogged down with words."*

SAM, THIRTY-TWO, ECONOMICS MAJOR AT SMITH COLLEGE, WENT BACK TO SCHOOL AFTER TEN YEARS OF BEING A PROFESSIONAL CHEF

"I agree. I don't consider myself a feminist because to do to so, include myself in one group or another, implies an exclusion. I really believe in attraction rather than promotion. Feminism is just a word; it has no power. To me it's all about action. I can't think my way into new behavior."

LANI (LEFT); SAM (RIGHT)

Lenelle

Lenelle Moïse, twenty-nine, was born in Port-au-Prince, Haiti, and came to Cambridge, Massachusetts, when she was two years old. She is a politically charged playwright, poet, and actress who travels all over the country to perform. Lenelle identifies as "culturally hyphenated" and "pomosexual." She has had tons of different influences from a young age. "I went to one of the most diverse high schools in the nation," she tells us. She describes her teenage self as "a theater geek with a flower child mentality in a fashionista body." Lenelle felt like an outcast in high school, telling us, "Most of my friends had no clue that I lived in the projects. I passed for middle class."

Lenelle says "yes" to being a feminist. "I recognize that racism, classism, heterosexism, and imperialism collaborate with sexism to keep a wide variety of people 'othered' and subordinated." Lenelle has been a feminist ever since seventh grade, when she joined a girl's empowerment group called the Sisters Program, founded by social worker and activist Julia Perez and other local Cambridge women. The word "feminist" never explicitly came up, but Lenelle sees these women as some of her first feminist influences.

I am curious to know if the rumors are true about Northampton—is it really the most lefty, feminist-friendly place on Earth? Lenelle seems

to think so. "When I was a graduate student at Smith, I rarely ran into students or professors who *didn't* identify as feminists," she remarks. "Most of my friends identify as either feminist or womanist. Even the dudes." As for her Haitian family, Lenelle says that they are proud of her. "I remember blowing my mother away when my partner and I came over and spent a few hours painting my little sister's bedroom. Working with the brushes and getting all sweaty and splattered was something so everyday for us, but it totally expanded her sense of what was possible." Lenelle challenges the men in her family all the time. They don't always see eye-to-eye, but "Haitians love a good debate," she says.

In the future, Lenelle wants to have more constructive dialogue with feminists who don't share her views and background—"I am so curious about the Condoleezza Rices of the world!" She also hopes that some "spirituality and self-care" creeps its way into activism and politics. "I've met a lot of burnt-out activists and bitter nonprofit workers who need more beauty and inspiration in their work environments, more laughter; activism can be sexy, lush, elegant, playful, dazzling, celebratory, ritualistic, and artful." Much to Emma's delight, Lenelle quotes her namesake: "Anarcha-feminist Emma Goldman said it best, 'If I can't dance, I don't want to be part of your revolution.'"

LENELLE

PROVINCETOWN

Emma's family traditionally goes to Provincetown every summer, and a talk with Emma's mom, a feminist painter, seems like a perfect way to round out our feminist art adventure. Somehow, though, it's more fitting to save her for last. In the meantime, we arrange an appointment with Byllye Avery, a longtime feminist activist for reproductive rights, while she's vacationing in Cape Cod.

Byllye

Byllye Avery meets with us on her porch, where her violets and posies are in full bloom. Byllye was born in Florida and feels that she has always been a feminist. "I always questioned why men had so much power, but I became aware of the word 'feminism' in the early '70s," she tells us. Byllye originally joined feminism through groups of white women, and in Florida in 1974 she opened the Gainesville Women's Health Center, one of the first that performed safe and legal abortions. At that time, "there were not very good feelings between white and black women—African American women really didn't want anything to do with white women's philosophies. A lot of women were turned off by the word 'feminism' due to white women's racism. Black women liked 'empowerment' better." Byllye adds that she always saw the value in the word "feminism" herself.

She later created the National Black Women's Health Project in 1981. It was then when Byllye realized that black women needed to come together to identify their own health issues. She found that

BYLLYE

"while African American women are willing to talk pretty much about anything—rape, abuse, domestic violence—very few of them talked about abortions. Women were, and still are, very guarded." This silence about reproductive health can be deadly, Byllye explains, especially when one takes into account the spread of AIDS and HIV among black women.

When it comes to young women, Byllye is worried that some of this history has been lost. She sees that some of the younger black women she works with are more willing to talk about reproductive health than their elders, but in terms of feminist identification, "It seems like we've gone kinda backwards. College women know about feminism, but everyday women in the streets don't. Those women don't have anyone talking to them at all." She notes that many young women—white women and women of color—don't even know what *Roe v. Wade* is. She feels that if the strength of feminist and reproductive activism is going to endure, it has to be updated by young women themselves, much in the way her generation did. "I'm always begging young women to please get on board and start defining these issues for their own generation."

Byllye acknowledges that a lot of the activism among young women happens online, but, like and Emma and me, she's not convinced that can substitute for real human interaction. "I don't know how to replace sitting across from someone who's been hurt, or who wants to talk about being raped or being a victim of sexual abuse," she says. "You can't reach through the computer and give them a hug. You can shut down that computer and move away."

Susan

We finally settle down with Susan Bee, Emma's mom, on a hot afternoon. Susan, like us, is a New Yorker to the core and has been a working artist there for decades. She is the coeditor with Mira Schor of the art journal *M/E/A/N/I/N/G*, and shows her work at A.I.R. Gallery, a New York City–based, women-only gallery with unapologetically feminist roots. Born in the '50s, Susan considers herself part of the "2.5" feminist wave— too young to be associated with the Second Wave but old enough to have been well-versed in feminism before the Third Wave. Her paintings and artist's books—rich with pin-ups, film noir, and pulp fiction imagery—play with gender issues. "I take that imagery made by men and make it my own," Susan explains.

Emma asks, "Do you definitely consider yourself a feminist artist even though it can be marginalizing?" "I think, yes," Susan says. "Because I'm a feminist and I'm an artist and I do a lot of artwork with women's imagery." "Does that make you a feminist artist rather than a feminist and an artist," Emma asks, "that your imagery is actually informed by feminism?" "I don't have a straight political answer to that question," her mother says. "In terms of art, the role of the imagination and fantasy and humor, of color—these are all important to me."

Emma's maternal grandmother, Miriam Laufer, was an artist and very involved with the feminist art movement. At Barnard, Susan became interested in being a women's studies major but couldn't pursue it because such a major didn't exist at that time. She even had trouble researching female artists. "I went to the stacks at Harvard," she tells us, "and tried to look up information about women artists for an art history paper. There wasn't any. Women's art history was being invented."

Susan tells us that virtually all her feminist artist friends at that time were childless. Then, when Susan was twenty-eight, her mother died suddenly, which set off Susan's desire to have a family. "I didn't really care about what feminists thought about it," she says. "I just incorporated Emma

SUSAN

into everything—the studio, the poetry readings, everything, just like my mom did with me." But she makes sure to emphasize the discrimination that a young artist mom experienced. It was so bad that "a lot of people hid their pregnancies and hid their children—it was such a career sinker." Emma was born in 1985, and Susan started *M/E/A/N/I/N/G* magazine in 1986. She was trying to get to the baby and to work and to her studio— it was really hard for her to run a magazine, too. Motherhood had bad career ramifications in the art world. Dealers told Susan that she would never work again, and they acted like mothers "had no brain power."

Kid-wise, things have improved a bit since the mid-'80s, but Susan echoes the concerns of Jeanne and the Brainstormers in New York: that dealers still simply do not want to show women artists. This kind of disparity is precisely the type of thing that incites some young feminists, and Susan sees some of that happening at A.I.R. "Kat Griefen," the new twenty-five-year-old director of the gallery, "is very profeminist." Some of her students "think it's something from the deep dark past that's kind of disreputable, and very humorless." She mentions that many mainstream women artists think feminism "is a word that can ruin their career."

The last bit of Susan's interview snaps us right back to reality. Until now, New England has conjured up memories of summers past, of frolicking in a comfy, lefty world where -isms weren't scary or off-putting. But these stories remind us yet again that for every self-identified feminist out there, there's another woman who's terrified of being marginalized, of being forever branded by a demonized history—even if she's doing amazing things for her fellow females.

Afterword

Since that last sunny day in Provincetown, Hillary Clinton has run for president and Sarah Palin has gone from being an unknown to a household name. We have a new president, Barack Obama, who has restored rights to stem-cell research, reversed the Global Gag Rule that blocked U.S. aid to other countries for abortion and birth control funding, and signed into law the Lilly Ledbetter Fair Pay Act of 2009. At the same time, the visibility and legitimacy of blogs and social networking sites has grown exponentially since we hit the road (if only Twitter had been as popular then as it is now!).

Obama was elected in part thanks to the staggering amount of support and mobilization of young people—including women—across the country. It feels as if the issues affecting both young people and women have been publicly debated, considered, and disseminated more in the last year than during all eight years of the Bush administration.

And yet the work we have to do is more important now than ever. How tragic would it be if those of us who got swept up in the momentum and change of the 2008 election season stopped what we're doing simply because we arrived at the door? Despite the glimmer of change, all the concerns of the women in these pages still manifest themselves every day. At this point, we have to encourage each other not just to name the problems and demand a fresh start but also to explore and discover how to change things while we're still riding the tidal wave.

And even though feminism and the issues associated with it have had recent spikes of exposure, the stereotypes around feminism that were voiced by countless women over the course of our trip are still going strong. Google the word and you'll still find links to scads of derisive, at times downright abusive, comment threads on highly trafficked blogs. You'll get websites like Feminism Is Evil, Ladies Against Feminism, and the extreme-right antiabortion organization Feminists for Life. The environment might have become intermittently more hospitable to these concepts and issues, but a major climate shift has yet to happen.

The good news is that our generation of young women cares about the future. No kidding, right? But twentysomethings get accused of apathy all the time. *Girldrive* has proven, if nothing else, that this is total bullshit. Whether they feel empowered, discouraged, enraged, or mobilized, young women have strong opinions and express them forcefully and eloquently. They don't all agree on *what* should happen for women in their lifetime, but virtually all of them want to see change. They may not call it "feminism," and may not feel they need the word, but it is crystal clear that young women are grappling with countless issues and problems related to their gender.

Okay, so we've determined that young women are doing awesome things. They're thinking critically, speaking their minds, and fighting for their future. Isn't this enough? Can't we scrap the word "feminism"? Emma's and my gut response has always been, Hell no. But aside from preserving the history, we could never figure out a cohesive way to explain why—and we didn't have the opportunity I'd always assumed we would to hash out our ideas in the final months of our project, to figure out what we wanted to say together as we headed into the home stretch of this joint project.

The day I sat down to write this epilogue, I happened upon an article called "The End of the Women's Movement," written by twenty-nine-year-old Courtney Martin, one of our New York interviewees. A time when there was a singular feminist agenda is "a time that has passed," she wrote. "Not only is the Women's Movement—as it was known in the 1960s—over, but women my age don't even agree on what a 'woman' really is." Yet Courtney wasn't bemoaning her generation's commitment to social change. On the contrary, she was applauding it. Gender-based activism now thrived through "strategic communication, alliance-building, and a million little grass-roots movements all over the country that fight for justice."

I saw in Courtney's words an articulation of exactly what Emma and I had witnessed during our months on the road. Feminism is no longer a movement the way it was in 1970s with Women's Liberation, or even in the 1990s with Riot Grrrl and the resurgence of "girl power" culture. Now that we've completed *Girldrive*, it's apparent—no, glaringly obvious—that young women don't want to get behind one or two central issues simply because they are women. This country is fucking huge, and so is the range of individual experience.

In reading Courtney's article, I also understood why Emma and I couldn't let go of the word "feminism." It was because we always saw the difference between using "feminism" as a call to collective action and using "feminism" to ignite an everyday gender consciousness. The word may be no longer necessary to label our generation's hardworking local and online activists—as Mandisa in New Orleans said, "Who cares? Just do the work!" If these women have come to a critical understanding of gender without using "feminism," great! Their awareness is what's important. But destigmatizing feminism is essential in a less tangible way: Not only does it make young women cognizant of issues relating to gender equality and justice but it also encourages them to consistently *talk about* these issues.

Midway through *Girldrive*, we determined a big difference between nonactivist women who called themselves feminists and women who didn't: Self-proclaimed feminists, beyond simply being aware of gender issues, discussed them all the time. The women who hadn't heard of feminism or weren't sure of its meaning had lots of things to say about their lives as females, but for many of them, it was the very first time they'd ever been asked such questions. Our hope in getting involved with a feminist project was always that feminism be framed as an amorphous, self-conscious state of mind to welcome or to leave alone rather than a loaded, combative ideology. We wanted to be involved in conversations that would in themselves function like grassroots activism—prompting women to talk about the way they understand their experience as women in this country—socially, politically, and economically. The more women talk, the more they can make informed decisions about their lives, their level of activism, and their relationships with people around them.

The biggest delay to social change is silence, and the biggest roadblock for the future is the erasure of history. Whether or not you personally embrace feminism, I hope that this book, in its depiction of so many faces of power, strength, integrity—and yes, feminism—will help you to consciously connect to a larger continuum and the ever-changing social reality around you. And of course, to the promise of discovery and happiness. Cause isn't that why feminism—and let's be real, road trips, too—were invented in the first place?

—**Nona**

Postscript

I press my foot on the gas, heart pounding. We are leaving Chicago, headed west. The steady beat of New Order begins the soundtrack of the movie we have seen a million times, but have never been in. Smiles spread like lightning across our faces. Our road trip has begun. We erase our minds, for a blank slate is the best state. We anticipate strange terrain. Unknown adventures and mishaps will shape every mile. The road tells us what to do. Scream, it says, throw your head out the window at one hundred miles an hour and let the wind whip against your face. Drive fearlessly through pitch black pouring rain, thick Midwestern morning fog. Gaze out the window. Notice the velvet black cows grazing on the ochre cornfields of Nebraska, snow capping the icy blue grand Tetons of Wyoming. Watch the fluorescent glow of fuchsia motel signs click off in the gray dawn, while sipping your complimentary coffee. Pull over to gawk at swirls of evergreen trees dipped in the brightest autumn hues, frosted with Montana mist. Every turn of the car brings a new excuse for dreamers. This is the rush of the road, seeing the highway stretch out endlessly and flipping it the bird. We are tirelessly moving forward and never lagging behind. Make the rules up as you go along. This must be what freedom feels like.

Every moment is fresh and vivid during this initial week on the road. We are opening our sleepy eyes from our world-weary slumber. While the language we used to describe our experiences was sincere, it was entrenched in a cinematic and literary idea of road tripping that we could not separate from own. Cultural amnesia followed us everywhere. "God, this is like that movie!" yet we could never remember the scene. Each philosophical musing was fraught with the stains of past travelers. Life imitated art in the most curious blend.

The American road trip is a charged symbol that we are taught to recognize from a young age. Whether it is the rebellious soul-searching of *On the Road* and *Thelma and Louise*, the colonial adventures of the Oregon Trail computer game or the capitalist dream of the Gold Rush, we have been trained to view road travel as an inherently American activity. Its inspirational power seems to penetrate every aspect of cultural production and collective memory. We think of '50s convertibles at the drive-in and James Dean's deadly game of chicken. There are the '60s VW vans following the Dead and covered in flower power, materialistic teenagers in the '80s obsessed with a red Corvette as the key to an independence located in trips to the mall or make-out lane. From the dysfunctional family trip to the Grand Canyon ("are we there yet?") to the proliferation of RV culture, we are a nation obsessed with vehicular myth.

But times have changed. The smog of LA ominously hangs over us. Giant SUVs guzzle blood for oil, tainting the innocence of the American roadtrip with the greed of the government. It is far more defiant to start a bike gang or study abroad then it is to celebrate the American landscape in a car. . . . This was part of the thrill of Nona and I deciding that we had to go on the road. I was sick of hating the unknown and wanted to try and get in touch with a horizon beyond my own self-imposed borders, even if that meant falling for a nostalgic notion of national identity. What we found defied our expectations. Hidden behind infinite glowing McDonald's arches on the highway was the sweet sight of something more. Every American legend seemed unwittingly alive through the gracious participation of small towns everywhere proudly interested in the preservation of their glorious past. This may be false historical memory, based on romanticized costume dramas and high school textbooks, but stumbling upon these strangely familiar architectural renderings of the past added a charmed mystique to our travels. The unassuming American landscape remained the easiest sight to inscribe with our newfound appreciation for our country. The unchanging grandeur of the national parks can inspire even the most cynical. At one point, we are zooming through the lush green fields of Iowa when, as on cue, Woody Guthrie's "This Land is Your Land" comes on the radio.

We fall into awed silence at the chorus: "This land is made for you and me." For a few minutes we forget our baggage and our Blackberry and melt into pools of optimism.

Generational identity is an outdated paradigm; we are too busy worrying about our personal survival to care. We are anonymous livejournal voices or local organizers. Some would say this disparate and desolate character is the locus of our collective voice. There is loneliness lurking behind every attempt we make to communicate through a world wide web. Lots of kids feel hopeless and useless to produce change in their own lives and beyond. The power of the road trip lies in the irreverence of doing something that exists as an end in itself. The search is supposed to be enough. Many of us no longer are given a chance to make moves in life that aren't documented, that don't only function as a stepping stone to something else. We couldn't even think of taking this road trip unless it took the form of an ambitious project!

. . . In our cultural folklore, women rarely go on the road, unless they are performing wild escapist fantasies, killing men, or abandoning their children as part of a confused menopausal midlife crisis. In *Thelma and Louise*, the pair didn't realize that they wanted freedom until it was too late. They had "snapped," projecting their anger onto every man they came across. Ours is not a tragic story of two women let down by a cruel, chauvinistic America. It is a story about two young women freshly released into the world as adults, imbued by an optimism uncharacteristic of our generation. Our trip marks is the fiftieth anniversary of the largely misogynistic *On the Road*, and *Girldrive* stands in defiance of this boys' club model of all-night chatter and roadside prostitution. Women are still relegated to the sidelines of intellectual and territorial exploration. We are warned against the dangers of venturing into the scary wild unknown, full of rapists and conman mechanics. Nona and I experienced our fair share of fear-inducing commentary before we left, the least of which was "Do you even know how to change a tire?"

For these reasons, feminism has always been inherently tied to travel and notions of self-discovery. It is not escape but ownership, reclaiming a space for investigation. Being exposed to the unfamiliar enriches our lives expands our ideas of what is possible. We need to look outside of ourselves to see ourselves. Feminism rests on the ability to characterize our experiences as part of a larger societal pattern. Feminist activism is about building cross-country and cultural networks that rely on the idea of intellectual travel.

After nearly a week of peaceful unpopulated landscapes, we were going to finally begin the daily slew of interviews that the route to Seattle to San Diego promised. The simple power of driving, of watching the terrain change, was now going to be mixed with faces and stories. Seascapes would mingle with skyscrapers to produce an untold American vista. As we rounded a corner on Route 5, I whispered, "Nona, this must be it! We must be on the West Coast." The blue water sparkled underneath the sinking sun, and the sandy mountains rose in the distance. This majestic entrance to Washington State was too good, too surreal. Did someone tell them we were coming? As we passed over the bridge entering Seattle, we felt the surge of anticipation and excitement that only seventy miles per hour at sunset can provide. The road tells you what to do. Throw on some shades, pump up the radio, put your hands on the wheel. Retrace your route in reflection, but look only as far as the blur of passing yellow lines to see the present. Race your future to the finish line.　　　**—Emma**

This essay was completed in Venice in December 2008. An extended version has been published in Emma's Belladonna book (see "Beyond Girldrive*").*

Nona's note: Emma and I didn't always agree, particularly on our generation's level of unity and optimism. She describes young people here as feeling isolated and powerless, overwhelmed by the blur of their own lives. For me, this sentiment never rang true, but Emma herself felt it deeply, which was also why *Girldrive* mattered so much to her. Disputes like these only affirmed the delicate head-and-heart balance of our partnership. Emma did admit, especially after the 2008 elections, that her perception of some young people's desolation didn't negate others' determination for change. But in the wake of her death, the fact that she wrote this essay seems to show her true ambivalence about the triumph of idealism over harsh realities.

Resources

An ulterior motive of *Girldrive* is to showcase what young women are inventing and involved in. Following is a list of the feminist or women-centered blogs, groups, projects, publications, and organizations mentioned in this book:

A.I.R. Gallery
www.airgallery.org

The Anarcha Project
www.anarcha.org

Big Star Burlesque
www.bigstarburlesque.com

Bitch magazine
http://bitchmagazine.org

Black Women's Health Imperative
www.blackwomenshealth.org

Brainstormers
www.brainstormersreport.net

Broad Vocabulary
abroadervocabulary.blogspot.com

Dirt Palace
www.dirtpalace.org

Feministe
www.feministe.us/blog

Feministing
www.feministing.com

Feminists for Progress
www.myspace.com/feministsforprogress

INCITE!
www.incite-national.org

Le Tigre
www.letigreworld.com

M/E/A/N/I/N/G Online
www.writing.upenn.edu/epc/meaning

NARAL
www.naral.org

Native American Women's Health Education Resource Center
www.nativeshop.org/nawherc.html

New Orleans Women's Health Clinic
nowhc.org

PODER (People Organized in Defense of Earth and her Resources)
www.poder-texas.org

Porn Perspectives (Rebecca's blog)
www.pornperspectives.com

Red River Women's Clinic
www.redriverwomensclinic.com

ROCKRGRL Magazine
www.rockrgrl.com

Royalty Media Group
royaltymedia.net

Step Up Women's Network
www.suwn.org

SwEEtie (Tecla's band)
www.myspace.com/sweetietheband

Third Wave Foundation
www.thirdwavefoundation.org

Translate Gender
www.translategender.org

V-Day and *The Vagina Monologues*
http://newsite.vday.org

Venus Zine
http://venuszine.com

What Would Thembi Do?
www.whatwouldthembido.com

Woman Made Gallery
www.womanmade.org

OTHER BLOGS BY, FOR, AND/OR ABOUT YOUNG FEMINISTS AND YOUNG WOMEN

Angry Black Bitch
http://angryblackbitch.blogspot.com

The Curvature
http://thecurvature.com

The F Bomb
http://thefbomb.org

HollaBackNYC (and in other cities, too)
www.hollabacknyc.blogspot.com

InHer City
www.hercity.org

Jezebel
http://jezebel.com

Pandagon
www.pandagon.net

The Pursuit of Harpyness
www.harpyness.com

What's Good for Girls
http://whatsgoodforgirls.blogspot.com

Womanist Musings
www.womanist-musings.com

Women, Girls, Ladies (intergenerational feminism)
http://womengirlsladies.blogspot.com

Women's Glib
http://womensglib.wordpress.com

JUST A SMATTERING OF OTHER FAVORITE FEMINIST BLOGS

Akimbo
http://blog.iwhc.org

Broadsheet
www.salon.com/mwt/broadsheet

Finally, a Feminism 101 Blog
http://finallyfeminism101.wordpress.com

Girl w/ Pen
www.girlwpen.com

RH Reality Check
www.rhrealitycheck.org

TransGriot
www.transgriot.blogspot.com

Viva La Feminista
www.vivalafeminista.com

Women & Hollywood
www.womenandhollywood.com

OTHER FEMINIST PUBLICATIONS AND ONLINE ZINES

Bitch
www.bitchmagazine.org

BUST
www.bust.com

ColorLines
www.colorlines.com

Damsel
www.damsel.typepad.com

Double X
www.doublex.com

The F-Word (UK)
www.thefword.org.uk/index

Hip Mama
www.hipmama.com

Ms.
www.msmagazine.com

Off Our Backs
www.offourbacks.org

For a directory of other women's and queer zines:
grrrlzines.net

YOUNG WOMEN/YOUNG FEMINIST ORGANIZATIONS

Association for Women's Rights in Development
www.awid.org

Center for Young Women's Development
www.cywd.org

Girls Inc.
www.girlsinc-online.org

Girls Write Now
www.girlswritenow.org/gwn

Feminist Majority Foundation, Feminist Campus
www.feministcampus.org/default.asp

FIERCE!
www.fiercenyc.org

Girls for a Change
www.girlsforachange.org

Girls for Gender Equity
www.ggenyc.info

National Council of Women's Organizations, Younger Women's Task Force
www.ywtf.org

Next GENDERation
www.nextgenderation.net

NOW, National NOW Young Women Task Force
www.now.org/issues/young/taskforce/index.html

Sistas on the Rise
www.sistasontherise.org

Third Wave Foundation
www.thirdwavefoundation.org

Women's Ordination Conference, Young Feminist Network
www.womensordination.org/content/view/13/40

Young Women's Empowerment Project
youarepriceless.org

Young Women's Project
www.youngwomensproject.org

FEMINISM/WOMEN IN THE MEDIA

Center for New Words
www.centerfornewwords.org

Feminist.com
www.feminist.com

Truthout
www.truthout.org

Women in Media & News (WIMN)
www.wimnonline.org

Women's eNews
www.womensenews.org

Women's Media Center
www.womensmediacenter.com

FINDING OTHER WOMEN'S ORGANIZATIONS

Feminist Majority Foundation Gateway
www.feminist.org/gateway/feministgateway-results.asp?category1=organizations

National Council for Research on Women
www.ncrw.org/about/centers.htm

National Council of Women's Organizations
www.womensorganizations.org

Photo Credits

Beyond Girldrive

Girldrive was never just a book. It was a journey, a blog, and a mini-movement. And just because the book is out doesn't mean all that has to stop.

While reading this book, you undoubtedly pondered some of the questions we asked hundreds of women across the country: *Do you consider yourself a feminist? What does feminism mean to you? What issues and topics are most important to you? What do you hope for the future?*

I encourage you to share these answers with me so I can share them with the world on www.girl-drive.com. On the site, I feature women we interviewed who are not featured in the book, as well as women who have sent in their thoughts. My hope is that your stories will continue the conversation, and that they'll even inspire a few more road trips!

Send your stories and photos to: nona@girl-drive.com.

On the site, you will also find a *Girldrive* FAQ and our original blog from the trip.

There are links to my writing at www.nonaswriting.com and more of Emma's photography at http://writing.upenn.edu/pepc/meaning/Bernstein.

After Emma's death, Belladonna published a book in her honor, featuring writing, photography, and interviews from *Girldrive*. Emma's Postscript also appears in the Belladonna book. You can order a copy at www.belladonnaseries.org.

A.I.R. Gallery, a feminist gallery in New York City where Emma's mother, Susan Bee, shows her work, has also named a fellowship in honor of Emma for an emerging and underrepresented woman artist under thirty. More information can be found at www.airgallery.org.

Acknowledgments

I am forever indebted to all two-hundred-plus women (and a few men) that gave up their time to bestow their words of wisdom upon us. Whether or not your interview made it into the book, every one of you is a piece of the heart and soul of *Girldrive*.

To our fairy godmothers Deborah Siegel, Jennifer Baumgardner, and Maria Buszek: Thanks for sharing your far-reaching connections, and for your generosity that reaches further still. Thank you to Feministing and Broadsheet—because of your early shout-outs, the word about *Girldrive* spread like wildfire.

An extra thank-you to our friends around the country who let us crash on their couches: Elena Herrada, Colleen Dilenschneider, Danya Shneyer, Sam Pitt-Stoller, Neil Dvorak, Liana Gomez, Mei-mei Berssenbrugge, Vanessa Greenfield and her hosts, Sean Abbott-Klafter and Nadiah Fellah, Mike Roberts and Anabel Bejerano, Emma Rosenbush and her housemates, Noah Melngailis, Noel Anderson and her housemates, Luke Anable, Szoke Schaeffer, Craig Klein and Angela Bennett, Caroline Knox, Fred Jameson and Susan Willis, Rachel Bleshman, Susan Bernstein, Lucille Songhai, Steve Dyer and Judith Shangold, and Camp Kinderland. An even more extra thank-you to these then–perfect strangers who hosted us: Julia Barry, Andrea Baumgarder and Brett Bernath, Melody Charles, the Dirt Palace artists, Nikki Giardina, Krista Jankowski, Leah from Sioux Falls, Becca Seely's parents, Shelby Melehes, and Jessica Vallelungo.

Our editor, Brooke Warner, was always the voice of reason when our heads were overflowing with disconnected ideas. Thanks for whipping *Girldrive* into shape. Thanks to our agent, Meredith Kaffel, who believed in this project before it was even a project. Thanks to all of our friends who helped out formally and informally to construct this book, like Sadye Vassil, Aaron Cassara, and all the other contributing photographers who picked up where Emma left off; like Collier Meyerson, who hashed out ideas with us on a regular basis in Chicago, New York, and Minnesota; and everybody who gave me love in the winter of '08/'09, which, thankfully, was *a lot* of people.

Thanks to Emma's parents, Susan Bee and Charles Bernstein, for sending photos and files and contributing to the editorial process in Emma's absence.

And thanks to my parents, Stanley Aronowitz and Ellen Willis—especially Mom, who inspired and propelled this project in so many ways.

—**Nona**

About the Authors

NONA WILLIS ARONOWITZ is a political and cultural critic born and raised in New York City. She has written about women, sex, music, technology, film, and youth culture for numerous publications including *The Nation, The New York Observer, The Village Voice,* and *Salon.* She graduated from Wesleyan University in 2006 with a degree in American studies. She now lives in Chicago and is a reporter and editor for the Tribune Company.

EMMA BEE BERNSTEIN was an artist and educator who grew up on the Upper West Side of Manhattan. She graduated June 2007 from the University of Chicago with degrees in visual arts and art history. She showed her photographs at A.I.R. Gallery in New York City, the Smart Museum of Art in Chicago, and in other student exhibitions at the University of Chicago. She worked as a teacher and docent for numerous museums, including the Art Institute of Chicago and the Museum of Contemporary Art. She died in Venice, Italy, in December 2008.

Selected Titles from Seal Press

For more than thirty years, Seal Press has published groundbreaking books. By women. For women. Visit our website at www.sealpress.com. Check out the Seal Press blog at www.sealpress.com/blog

Full Frontal Feminism: A Young Woman's Guide to Why Feminism Matters, BY JESSICA VALENTI. $15.95, 1-58005-201-0. *A sassy and in-your-face look at contemporary feminism for women of all ages.*

Laid: Young People's Experiences with Sex in an Easy-Access Culture, EDITED BY SHANNON T. BOODRAM. $15.95, 1-58005-295-9. *This hard-hitting anthology paints a candid portrait of what sex is like—the good and the bad—for today's young people.*

Hellions: Pop Culture's Rebel Women, BY MARIA RAHA. $15.95, 1-58005-240-1. *Maria Raha, author of Cinderella's Big Score, analyzes women ranging from Marilyn Monroe to the reality TV stars of the twenty-first century in an effort to redefine the notion of female rebellion.*

Rock Your Stars: Your Astrological Guide to Getting It All, BY HOLIDAY MATHIS. $15.95, 1-58005-217-7. *In the lively and intelligent Rock Your Stars, syndicated columnist and "rock 'n' roll astrologer" Holiday Mathis offers a modern manual to making every life decision, whether it's what to wear, who to love, which career ladder to climb, what color to paint the bedroom, or how to find the right exercise plan—all by using astrology as a practical guide.*

Bento Box In the Heartland: My Japanese Girlhood in Whitebread America, BY LINDA FURIYA. $15.95, 1-58005-191-X. *A uniquely American story about girlhood, identity, assimilation—and the love of homemade food.*

Chick Flick Road Kill: A Behind the Scenes Odyssey into Movie-Made America, BY ALICIA REBENSDORF. $15.95, 1-58005-194-4. *A twentysomething's love-hate relationship with picture-perfect Hollywood sends her on a road trip in search of a more real America.*